Restorative Policing Experiment

The Bethlehem Pennsylvania Police Family Group Conferencing Project

Paul McCold, Ph.D.
&
Benjamin Wachtel

WIPF & STOCK · Eugene, Oregon

Wipf and Stock Publishers
199 W 8th Ave, Suite 3
Eugene, OR 97401

Restorative Policing Experiment
The Bethlehem Pennsylvania Police Family Group Conferencing Project
By McCold, Paul and Wachtel, Benjamin
Copyright©1998 by McCold, Paul
ISBN 13: 978-1-62032-384-7
Publication date 8/1/2012
Previously published by Community Service Foundation, 1998

Acknowledgments

The authors gratefully acknowledge the following individuals for their contributions to this project:

Captain John Stahr, Project Liaison, Bethlehem Police Department, without whom this study would not have been possible. John provided the operational and motivational support responsible for Operation P.R.O.J.E.C.T.

Ted Wachtel, Executive Director, Community Service Foundation, for his collaboration in launching the Restorative Policing Experiment and for providing the essentials of office space and support.

Police Commissioner Eugene Learn, former Police Commissioner John W. Yerk and the Bethlehem Police Department, for their assistance and ongoing support and cooperation.

The Restorative Policing Experiment research advisory board, for their valuable input and guidance:
- Howard Zehr, Director, Office of Criminal Justice, Mennonite Central Committee
- James Anderson, Executive Director, Pennsylvania Juvenile Court Judges Commission
- Ruth Williams, Juvenile Justice Program Manager, Pennsylvania Commission on Crime and Delinquency
- Ronald Sharp, Director of Psychological Services, Alternative Rehabilitation Communities
- Henry Sontheimer, Senior Evaluation Analyst, Pennsylvania Commission on Crime and Delinquency
- Philip Harris, Professor of Criminal Justice, Temple University
- Mary Achilles, Pennsylvania Victim Advocate and Director of Victim Services, Pennsylvania Department of Corrections

Sergeant Terry O'Connell, New South Wales Police Service, master facilitator and the father of restorative policing, whose standards for conferencing formed the basis of the program protocol used in this research.

John Braithwaite and Heather Strang, Australia National University, Lawrence Sherman, University of Maryland, and the enthusiastic RISE researchers and advisors for their generous sharing of research instruments and for providing invaluable insights and support into our project's implementation and analyses.

The **REAL** JUSTICE team for their daily support and technical expertise and for their ongoing success in putting what they preach into practice.

Mark Umbreit, Center for Restorative Justice & Mediation, for his pioneering work evaluating mediation, which set a high standard for restorative justice research. Mark's work made this study's comparisons of conferencing with VOM possible.

Captain Phillip Richardson, Bethlehem Police Department; Nick Melnick, Electronic Data Interchange Coordinator, Administrative Office of Pennsylvania Courts; and the staff at Northampton County and Lehigh County Juvenile Probation for their assistance in data collection.

Criminal justice officials from Lehigh and Northampton counties for their support and cooperation:
- Judge William Moran, Northampton County
- Judge Edward Reibman, Lehigh County
- John Morganelli, Northampton County District Attorney
- Robert Steinberg, former Lehigh County District Attorney
- Dennis Galligani, Chief, Northampton County Juvenile Probation
- Paul Werrell, Chief, Lehigh County Juvenile Probation
- Nancy Matos-Gonzalez, District Justice, Bethlehem
- Elizabeth Romig, District Justice, Bethlehem
- Barbara Schlegel, District Justice, Bethlehem
- James Stocklas, District Justice, Bethlehem
- Thomas Murphy, District Justice, Bethlehem

ABSTRACT

This is a report on the Bethlehem Pennsylvania Police Family Group Conferencing Project. First-time moderately serious juvenile offenders were randomly assigned either to formal adjudication or to a diversionary "restorative policing" process called family group conferencing. Police-based family group conferencing employs trained police officers to facilitate a meeting attended by juvenile offenders, their victims, and their respective family and friends, to discuss the harm caused by the offender's actions and to develop an agreement to repair the harm. Victim and offender participation is voluntary. The effect of the program was measured through surveys of victims, offenders, offender's parents and police officers and by examining outcomes of conferences and formal adjudication. Results are related to six questions about restorative policing. Findings include: 42% participation rate, 100% of conferences (n=67) reaching an agreement, 94% of offenders (n=80) fully complying with agreements, and participant satisfaction and sense of fairness exceeding 96%. Results suggests that recidivism was more a function of offenders choice to participate than the effects of the conferencing, per se. Violent offenders participating in conferences had lower rearrest rates than violent offenders declining to participate, but this was not true for property offenders.

Table of Contents

EXECUTIVE SUMMARY 1

1. RESTORATIVE POLICING 7

2. THE BETHLEHEM EXPERIMENT 15

3. CONFERENCE OBSERVATIONS 27

4. POLICE SURVEYS 39

5. PARTICIPANT SURVEYS 47
    VICTIM SURVEY RESULTS 51
    OFFENDER SURVEY RESULTS 58
    PARENT SURVEY RESULTS 64

6. RECIDIVISM 73

7. SYSTEMIC RESPONSES 79

8. COMPARATIVE ANALYSES 89

9. CONCLUSIONS 103
    LIMITATIONS OF CURRENT RESEARCH 110

APPENDICES 115

ENDNOTES 137

List of Exhibits

Exhibits	page #

Summary

Exhibit S1: Satisfaction with handling of case 5

Exhibit S2: Participation rate comparison with VOM 6

Technical Report

The Bethlehem Experiment

Exhibit 1: Proportion of total juvenile arrests disqualified from study 18

Exhibit 2: Offender eligibility categories 18

Exhibit 3: Random assignment results - Cases 19

Exhibit 4: Random assignment results - Offenders 19

Exhibit 5: Treatment group participation rates 19

Exhibit 6: Arrest charges for offenders included in study by experimental group 20

Exhibit 7: Arrest charge categories for offenders included in study
 by experimental group 20

Exhibit 8: Experimental group comparisons 21

Exhibit 9a: Reasons for cases declining to participate 22

Exhibit 9b: Corrected Participation Rates 22

Exhibit 10: Participation rates of treatment-selected offenders 23

Exhibit 11: Offender case disposition by crime type and control group 24

Exhibit 12: Magistrate findings for cases in study disposed by magistrate court 24

Conference Observations

Exhibit 13: Type of victims 29

Exhibit 14: Mean number of inappropriate coordinator responses
 by period of experiment 31

Exhibit 15: Mean score for distinguishing deed from doer by period of experiment 31

Exhibit 16: Mean facilitator grade by period of experiment 32

Exhibit 17: Mean coordinator grade by conference sequence 33

Exhibit 18: Mean number of participants by conference sequence 33

Exhibit 19: Observer ratings of most punitive participant 35

Exhibit 20: Conference agreement terms 35

Exhibit 21: Average restitution for cases agreeing to restitution 37

Police Surveys

Exhibit 22: Reliability of Hassles and Uplifts Scales 41-42
Exhibit 23: Police attitude scales reliability 41
Exhibit 24: Police orientation scales reliability 42
Exhibit 25: Conferencing scales reliability 43
Exhibit 26: Police survey response rates 44
Exhibit 27: Knowledge of conferencing by experimental period 45
Exhibit 28: Mean change in orientation toward the use of force 45
Exhibit 29: Mean change in perception of community cooperation 46
Exhibit 30: Mean change in crime control orientation 46

Participant Surveys

Exhibit 31: Case dispositions of offenders in study 47
Exhibit 32: Participant survey response rates 50
Exhibit 33: Victim satisfaction 52
Exhibit 34: Victims experiencing fairness 52
Exhibit 35: Victims agreeing offender was held accountable 52
Exhibit 36: Victims agreeing their opinion was considered 52
Exhibit 37: Court victims attitudes toward offense and offender 53
Exhibit 38: Conferenced victims perceptions 54
Exhibit 39: Conferenced victims agreeing with statements about conferencing 55
Exhibit 40: Importance of issues for victims 56
Exhibit 41: Offender satisfaction 59
Exhibit 42: Offender attitude toward victim 60
Exhibit 43: Court offenders attitudes toward victims 60
Exhibit 44: Conference offenders perceptions of conferencing 61
Exhibit 45: Conferenced offenders attitudes toward conferencing 62
Exhibit 46: Importance of issues for offenders 62
Exhibit 47: Offender's parent satisfaction 65
Exhibit 48: Offender's parents reporting sense of fairness 65
Exhibit 49: Offender's parents agreeing their opinion was considered 66
Exhibit 50: Offender's parents attitudes toward conferencing 67
Exhibit 51: Offender's parents perceptions of conferencing 68
Exhibit 52: Importance of issues for offender's parents 69

Offender Recidivism

Exhibit 53: Rearrest rates by days of exposure by crime type 75-76
Exhibit 54a: Rearrest rates for violent offenders 76
Exhibit 54b: Rearrest rates for property offenders 76
Exhibit 55: Rearrest rates for offenders declining to participate
            by reasons for decline 77

Systemic Responses

Exhibit 56: Monthly juvenile arrests 80

Exhibit 57: Juvenile arrests 1995 to 10/1997 80

Exhibit 58: Proportion of eligible cases selected during experimental period 81

Exhibit 59a: Rearrest rates - all eligible property offenders 82

Exhibit 59b: Rearrest rates - all eligible violent offenders 82

Exhibit 60: Rearrest rates - total juvenile arrests by crime 83

Exhibit 61a: Rearrest rates - property offenders by eligibility category 83

Exhibit 61b: Rearrest rates - violent offenders by eligibility category 84

Exhibit 62: Total juvenile arrests by experimental period by eligibility category 84

Exhibit 63: Non-selected eligible and selected juvenile arrests by month 85

Exhibit 64: Arrests handled informally and selected arrests by month 85

Exhibit 65: Disposition of eligible cases by experimental period 85

Exhibit 66: Disposition of cases not in study by experimental period 86

Exhibit 67: Percent payment ordered magistrate cases by experimental period 86

Exhibit 68: Mean payment ordered - magistrate cases by experimental period 86

Exhibit 69: Disposition comparison - magistrate cases
    by inclusion status and crime type 86

Exhibit 70: Percent payment ordered - magistrate cases
    by inclusion status and crime type 87

Exhibit 71: Mean payment ordered - magistrate cases by experimental period 87

Comparative Analysis

Exhibit 72: Disposition of court-assigned cases in study 93

Exhibit 73: Percent of cases disposed via guilty plea 93

Exhibit 74: Proportion of offenders paying monetary costs by treatment group 94

Exhibit 75: Mean monetary costs for offenders paying costs 95

Exhibit 76: Participation rates comparison to VOM 95

Exhibit 77: Victim satisfaction comparison to VOM 96

Exhibit 78: Offender satisfaction comparison to VOM 96

Exhibit 79: Victim sense of fairness comparison to VOM 97

Exhibit 80: Offender sense of fairness comparison to VOM 97

Exhibit 81: Crime victim's ratings of process comparison to VOM 99

Exhibit 82: Criminal offender's ratings of process comparison to VOM 99

Exhibit 83: Unit cost comparison to VOM 100

Restorative Justice Classics Series Foreword

The phrase "restorative justice" was unknown before the 1970s. Forty years later restorative justice is a vast international movement: nearly a million pages on the Internet refer to it; Google Scholar lists 16,600 books and essays on restorative justice; many states around the world have written it into law; and more important, hundreds of thousands of people and communities have had their fear and shame transformed by encounters with and efforts of those practicing restorative justice.

Along the way, while having intentions to repair harm, restorative justice initiatives have also added to harm. The growth of this mass movement is not without missteps and failures, some very painful. If this movement is to be advanced wisely into the future, its advocates need to remember both fruitful attempts and painful ones.

The Restorative Justice Classics Series is an attempt to help create foundations and share memories for those interested in restorative justice. In a movement that grows and changes so incredibly fast and in so many diverse places, this book series creates space for cultivating restorative justice memory. Amidst the frenzy of work, growth, and missteps, this book series represents a commitment to bring back into print those restorative justice books and articles that could be considered classic. The label "classic" is used here loosely to refer to books that have shaped the restorative justice movement and whose writing continues to be worth remembering, worth sharing, and worth reconsidering amidst the changing scene. In most cases there is still a need for the content and thus a continuing demand for the books.

Books are chosen in this series because they will be of special ongoing value to practitioners and scholars of restorative justice. Wipf and Stock Publishers, at the instigation of Series Editor Ted Lewis, has set up the series in such a way that the books will stay in print and remain available. Anyone wanting to understand the origins, history, diverse practices, and spirit of restorative justice will find the series particularly helpful.

Jarem Sawatsky, Series Consultant
Canadian Mennonite University
Winnipeg, Manitoba
April 2009

To see a complete listing of books in this series, go to www.wipfandstock.com and click on "Advanced Search" to locate the Restorative Justice Classics Series in the series box. Recommendations for further reprints in this series can be directed to Ted Lewis, Series Editor, at tedlewis@wipfandstock.com or can be made by calling 541-344-1528.

RESTORATIVE POLICING EXPERIMENT
Bethlehem Pennsylvania Police Family Group Conferencing Project*

EXECUTIVE SUMMARY

Restorative justice is the latest trend in criminal justice practice that contains the seeds of a radically different paradigm on crime and justice than the traditional deterrence or desert-based approaches. This report is an evaluation of one restorative justice program operated by the police in Bethlehem, Pennsylvania, a mid-sized American city whose justice practices are typical of thousands of such communities across the country.

Although developed independently from the restorative justice movement, family group conferencing is considered an important new development in restorative justice practice as a means of dealing more effectively with young offenders by diverting them from court and involving their extended families and victims in addressing their wrongdoing. Originating in New Zealand in 1989, conferencing was substantially revised as a community policing technique in Wagga Wagga, New South Wales, Australia, in 1991. This was the first program to directly involve a justice official in conducting restorative justice, and has since broadened to include school officials, probation officers and others. The "Wagga model" was introduced to North America in 1995 by the Real Justice® organization, and more than 2,000 police, probation officers, educators and others in the United States and Canada have now been trained as conference facilitators.

Purpose

The Bethlehem Pennsylvania Police Family Group Conferencing Project was designed to answer six programmatic questions about police-based conferencing as it is being applied in the United States.

1. Can typical American police officers conduct conferences consistent with due process and restorative justice principles?
2. Does involvement in conferencing transform police attitudes, organizational culture and role perceptions?
3. Does conferencing produce conflict-reducing outcomes by helping to solve ongoing problems and reduce recidivism?
4. Will victims, offenders and the community accept a police-based restorative justice response?
5. Does the introduction of diversionary conferencing alter the case processing of juvenile offenders (e.g., net-widening)?
6. How does police-based conferencing compare to the existing system and to other restorative justice practices?

*This project was supported under award number 95-IJ-CX-0042 from the National Institute of Justice, Office of Justice Programs, U.S. Department of Justice. Points of view in this document are those of the authors and do not necessarily represent the official position of the U.S. Department of Justice.

Methods

In October 1995, 20 full-time police officers volunteered to be trained and conduct conferences. Over an 18-month period, first-time juvenile offenders arrested for selected misdemeanor and summary offenses were randomly assigned either to formal adjudication or to a diversionary restorative policing conference. Cases were blocked by crime type: crimes primarily directed against the person (violent offenses) and crimes primarily directed against property (property offenses).

The effect of the program was measured through surveys of victims, offenders and offenders' parents. Additional data was obtained from direct observations of conferences and review of official police and court records. Two department-wide surveys were conducted, prior to the first conference and again after 18 months of program operation. Officer attitudes on a wide range of questions about their work environment and the nature of policing were matched by officer for pre- and post-test comparisons.

During the course of the experiment, 215 criminal incidents involving the arrests of 292 juveniles qualified for the study, representing 23% of all juvenile offenders arrested in Bethlehem during the time period. These included 75 violent crimes and 140 property crimes. A store was the victim in 76% of the property cases and a school was the victim in 29% of the violent cases.

Participation in the program was voluntary, creating three groups of subjects: (1) statistical control group (n=68 property, 35 violent), (2) selected for conferencing and participating (n=56 property, 24 violent), and (3) selected for conferencing but not participating (n=57 property, 52 violent). Conferences for violent offenses were conducted in 32% of cases selected for the treatment group, and in 50% of property cases, for an overall raw participation rate of 42% (proportion of conferences to cases selected). Offenders were much more likely to decline in property offenses and victims more likely in violent offenses. Among crime seriousness, number of charges, age, race, and gender of offender, only gender was significantly related to participation rate, and only among violent offenders with females participating at twice the rate as their male counterparts.

In spite of the probable self-selection bias in the treatment group, the generalizability of the sample was maintained. However, for this experiment to demonstrate a recidivism reduction or an improvement over magistrate court cases, differences had to be strong enough to be measured across the entire treatment-selected group, even though less than half received the treatment. Questions about how police conducted conferences, whether this affected their culture, whether the community will accept the program, and how the program affected case processing do not require equivalent comparison groups and are unaffected by the threat to the internal validity of the experimental design.

Results

1. Can typical American police officers conduct conferences consistent with due process and restorative justice principles?

There was an initial tendency among some officers to lecture the offender or influence the agreement in conferences. While they easily picked up the mechanics of the scripted process, an additional in-service training was necessary early in the experiment to reinforce the reintegrative intention of conferences. Average grades for overall compliance with protocol improved significantly following the in-service training, from 80% to 89%.

In general, officers did a sufficient but not exemplary job in adhering to principles of restorative justice and ensuring due process. In spite of this, more than 96% of participants said they were satisfied with how their cases were handled and perceived the process as fair, more than 94% would choose to do the conference again, and more than 92% would recommend conferences to others. These results, which are consistent with the earlier evaluation of police conferencing in Australia, lend support to the generalizability of the Australian findings to police-based conferencing in the United States.

2. Does conferencing transform police attitudes, organizational culture and role perceptions?

There were no significant changes in overall police attitudes, organizational culture or role perceptions. Paired t-tests of pre- and post-test scores failed to detect any department-wide changes in attitudes during the experimental period. Thus, conferencing cannot be said to have had a significant impact on changing overall police attitudes toward their activities or the role of police.

The officers who had conducted conferences did show a significant increase in their perceptions of community cooperation and a decrease in their orientation toward a crime control approach to policing. Thus the whole effect of conferencing was to cause a few officers who were positively disposed to community policing to become more supportive of such approaches.

3. Does conferencing produce conflict-reducing outcomes by helping to solve ongoing problems and reduce recidivism?

Reducing offender recidivism is one measure of the capacity of restorative approaches to address the important needs created by a criminal offense. A reduction in re-offending is not the primary purpose, as in deterrence theory, but is one of a number of goals for the restorative response to crime. It is assumed that holding offenders accountable to their victims to repair the harm caused should increase offender empathy and thereby lead to a reduction in offending behavior.

Results indicate that lower recidivism for those participating in the program was more a function of the offender's choice to participate than the effects of the conference, per se. Violent offenders participating in conferences had significantly lower 12-month rearrest rates (20%) than those who declined to participate (48%). However, the control group rearrest rate (35%) was almost exactly between the treatment-selected groups, indicating that there was little additional treatment effect beyond a self-selection effect. Recidivism rates for the property offenders suggests that any self-selection effect was transitory. There were significant differences for the decline and conference property offenders from 30 to 150 days, however, these differences in the rearrest rates were not significant by 12 months.

The universal ability of conference participants to come up with mutually acceptable agreements demonstrates that conferences are useful in facilitating a collective, community-based solution to these criminal problems. The 94% offender compliance with the terms of the agreements supports the conclusion that these cases were resolved in a manner satisfactory to all participants.

It appears that any reductions in recidivism are the result of the voluntary program diverting from formal processing those juveniles who are least likely to re-offend in the first place. Presumably this is the goal of any good diversion program and, in this regard, the program was successful.

4. Will victims, offenders and the community accept a police-based restorative justice response?

Victims participating in conferences said that they felt participating in the conference was their own choice (96%); they would recommend conferences to others (92%); they would choose a conference if they had to do it over again (94%); meeting with the offender was helpful (93%); the tone of the conference was basically friendly (94%); the offender apologized (96%); and conferences should be offered to all victims (81%).

Offenders who participated in conferences said that it was their own choice to participate (92%); they would recommend conferencing to others (92%); if they had to do it over again, they would choose to participate (94%); meeting with the victim was helpful (100%); and the tone of the conference was friendly (96%).

Nearly all parents of conferenced offenders said they would recommend conferencing to others (97%), would choose to participate in a conference if they had to do it over again (94%), thought that meeting the victim was helpful (97%), and that they had a positive or very positive attitude toward the conference (91%).

Victims, offenders and parents of offenders were consistently satisfied with the conferencing process and perceived the process and the outcomes as fair. Nearly all respondents indicated they would choose to participate in the program again and would recommend it to others facing similar trouble. While a majority of offenders declined to participate, a very high proportion of victims, offenders and offenders' parents who did participate accepted this police-based restorative justice process.

5. How does the introduction of conferencing alter the case processing of juvenile offenders?

There was no apparent change in overall arrest patterns for juvenile offenders during the experimental period. A gradual decline in juvenile arrests throughout the period began before the police started conducting diversionary conferences. The time series for the cases disposed of informally during the study showed no disruption from the pattern prior to the experiment, and this is the pool of offenders who would have been affected by net-widening. Because offenders were selected for this study after they had already been arrested, there was no discretion on the part of officers to determine which cases would be referred. Thus, there really was no opportunity for net-widening.

Dispositions of offenders three years prior to the study were compared to those handled by court during the period of the study and there were no important differences evident. Offenders diverted tended to be less serious cases and were likely to have entered a guilty plea if the case had gone to court, thus slightly increasing the average seriousness of the cases remaining in the system. Overall case processing of juvenile offenders by police and the courts was largely unaffected by the existence of the program.

6. How does conferencing compare to the existing system and to other restorative justice practices?

Existing System

Victims, offenders and offenders' parents who participated in a conference were at least as satisfied with the way their case was handled and to have experienced fairness as those whose cases were processed through court (Exhibit S1). Victims and parents were more likely to feel that their opinion had been adequately considered. There were no significant differences between the control and treatment (decline and conference combined) victims for the satisfaction, fairness, accountability and opinion items. Among property crime victims, there was a significant difference: the treatment group was more likely to say the offender was adequately held accountable for the offense.

Sixty-three percent of conferenced offenders said they were very satisfied with the way their case was handled, compared to 34% of the control group and 24% of the decline group. Similarly, parents were also more likely to say they were very satisfied with the conference compared to the control or decline group parents. Parents of conferenced youth were more likely to report fairness in their child's case than those disposed by courts. Still, a majority of all parents in the survey experienced fairness with the handling of their child's case.

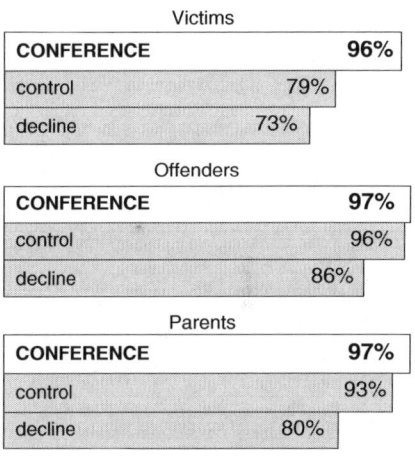

Exhibit S1. Satisfaction with handling of case

Conferenced parents were more likely to have felt their opinion had been adequately considered in their child's case than parents of court-disposed offenders: 92% of the conference group, 84% of the control group, and 55% of the decline group.

Police-based conferencing produced outcomes for offenders more specifically tailored to the individual's circumstances than the court process, especially for violent cases with personal victims. Outcomes from conferences were more likely to include community service as a reparative response and less likely to require monetary payments than outcomes from the courts.

Restorative Justice Programs

Other than conferencing, the primary restorative justice program for which there is research is victim-offender mediation (VOM). Participant questionnaires for the present study were designed from those asked in a majority of the VOM evaluations. There are a number of differences between conferencing and mediation, though both utilize a voluntary collaborative model with the purpose of repairing the harm caused by the crime. Individual VOM programs also vary regarding the type of cases qualifying and the source of administration and case referral sources.

Police-based conferences in the present study produced participant results and program participation rates higher than any of the reported VOM programs (Exhibit S2). The agreement compliance rates in the Bethlehem study are comparable to those cited in other mediation and conferencing studies. In light of these findings, concerns raised by VOM advocates that victims and offenders would be less trusting of police than of impartial community volunteers seem unfounded.

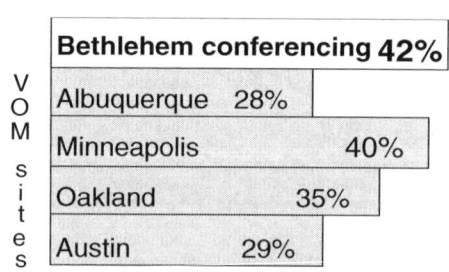

Exhibit S2. Particiation rate comparison with VOM

Finally, crude cost comparisons suggest that police-based conferencing is no more expensive than any of the VOM programs compared. Because police conduct conferences as part of their routine community policing activities, there were no additional program costs to the department beyond initial training costs.

General Conclusions

In summary, the following general conclusions can be made:
- Typical American police officers are capable of conducting conferences consistent with due process and restorative justice principles, given adequate training and supervision.
- While conferencing did not transform police attitudes, organization culture or role perceptions, it did move those with the most exposure to conferencing toward a more community-oriented, problem-solving stance.
- Police-facilitated restorative conferences can produce conflict-reducing outcomes, most clearly in cases of interpersonal violence. Because of a strong self-selection bias, this study could not confirm a reduction in recidivism due to conferencing. Like other voluntary diversion programs, cooperative cases participated, uncooperative cases did not.
- Victims, offenders and parents who participated accepted this police-based restorative justice response, as indicated by high rates of satisfaction with the process and experiences of fairness.
- Police-facilitated restorative conferences produced participant satisfaction and perceptions of fairness at least as high as other restorative justice programs and the courts. Participation rates and compliance rates for conferences were also comparable to other restorative justice programs.

1
Restorative Policing

This is a report on the Bethlehem Pennsylvania Police Family Group Conferencing Project, National Institute of Justice research grant.* Juvenile offenders who qualified for the study were randomly assigned either to formal adjudication or to a diversionary "restorative policing" process called family group conferencing. Police-based family group conferencing employs trained police officers to facilitate a meeting attended by juvenile offenders, their victims, and their respective family and friends, to discuss the harm caused by the offender's actions and to develop a plan to repair the harm. Victim and offender participation is voluntary. The effect of the program was measured through surveys of victims, offenders, offender's parents and police officers and by examining outcomes of conferences and formal adjudication.

Family group conferencing (also called community conferencing) originated in New Zealand in 1989 under the auspices of the social welfare department as a means of diverting young offenders from formal adjudication. Conferencing was substantially revised and pioneered as a community policing technique in Wagga Wagga, New South Wales, Australia in 1991 (Moore and McDonald, 1995). The "Wagga model" was introduced to North America in 1995 by the REAL JUSTICE® organization, and more than 2,000 police, probation officers, educators and others in the United States and Canada have been trained as conference facilitators (Umbreit and Zehr, 1996; Wachtel, 1995).

Police-based conferencing provides a forum for the police to bring together juvenile offenders and their victims with their respective families and supporters. This microcommunity of citizens directly affected by the crime collectively seeks resolution of the injuries, which may include apology, reparation to the victim, and reintegration of the offender. Ideally, solutions are not imposed by the facilitator, but instead result from the dynamic interaction of participants. Goals of the conference are: to encourage young offenders to achieve empathy toward their victims and take responsibility for their crimes, allow victims to move toward forgiveness and healing, and empower citizens to appropriately address their own local problems (McCold, 1997; Moore and O'Connell, 1994).

The practice of restorative policing is related to three trends in re-examining the Western system of justice: 1) community policing and problem-oriented policing (Goldstein, 1990); 2) reintegrative shaming theory (Braithwaite, 1989); and 3) restorative justice (Zehr, 1990; McCold, 1997a).

---

*This project was supported under award number 95-IJ-CX-0042 from the National Institute of Justice, Office of Justice Programs, U.S. Department of Justice. Points of view in this document are those of the authors and do not necessarily represent the official position of the U.S. Department of Justice.

Community and Problem-Oriented Policing

Conferencing is more consistent with Herman Goldstein's definition of problem-oriented policing than with the vague and varied notions of community policing often set forth by practitioners and researchers. Community policing means many different things to different people (Hunter and Barker, 1993; Bayley, 1994). There is some consensus that its general aims are to prevent crime and create a better quality of life and to change the reactive, control-oriented style of policing to a proactive, problem-solving, service-oriented style. The stated objectives of community policing, however, are varied: to reduce crime, fear of crime, calls for service and complaints against police; to increase preventative knowledge, crime clearance rates, public satisfaction, number of volunteers, police satisfaction, efficiency and effectiveness; and to build police-community partnerships (Normandeau, 1993). The specific methods of achieving these aims may differ very little from previous policing approaches, and despite its popularity, community policing is described as "more rhetoric than reality" (Mastrofski, 1988; Klockars, 1988; Jones et al., 1994; Bull & Stratta, 1994; Stenson, 1993).

Herman Goldstein, considered by many to be "the father of problem-oriented policing," differentiates between community policing and problem-oriented policing. He says that community policing is "designed to place great emphasis on one great need in policing, which is to engage the community" (1997, p.8); problem-oriented policing has a broader focus—to adopt an analytical approach to identify and solve the specific problems that police confront. A key element in this is intensively engaging the community in problem solving (Goldstein, 1990; 1997).

Goldstein argues that the job of social control in society ultimately depends upon networks other than the police, networks that the police can only facilitate and support. The community should become responsible for policing itself:

> Several arguments can be made for maximum use of informal controls that are already available in the community. First, invoking informal nongovernmental control may truly be the most effective means for dealing with the problem. Second, doing so reinforces the concept of the police as facilitators in getting the community to control itself rather than depending on the police and the criminal justice system for control. Third, it supports the strong preference, when an option exists, for using the least restrictive, least intrusive method of dealing with a problem. (Goldstein, 1990, p.121).

Goldstein offers numerous examples of police mobilizing the community and making use of existing forms of informal social controls, such as: involving citizens in developing solutions to specific crime problems; promoting interaction among populations of varying age and racial composition to reduce fear; holding meetings to resolve ongoing conflicts among neighborhood residents; and seeking the help of "those who, because they have some power over an individual, may be able to influence his or her behavior" (1990, p.121).

Goldstein claims that individual police tend to have a clear definition of community:

> In what I have observed of the practice, as distinct from the rhetoric of community policing, police tend to engage the citizenry in a very pragmatic and more relaxed manner. They use "community" rather deftly to describe those affected in any way by the specific problem they are attempting to address, or the program being launched in response to the problem. (1990, p.25)

It is the involvement of the micro-community of those affected by a specific crime in providing informal social control and developing a mutually acceptable plan for resolution that makes family group conferencing consistent with Goldstein's view of problem-oriented policing.

Reintegrative Shaming Theory

John Braithwaite's (1989) theory of reintegrative shaming contributed to the development of the Wagga model of conferencing. This theory about the causes of crime in societies has two parts. The first part suggests that the manner in which a society handles the emotion of shame will determine its degree of crime and violence. When shame is used to humiliate or stigmatize, those who are stigmatized will seek out criminal subcultures where they can find positive self-images. According to the theory, there is a positive relationship in societies between the intensity of stigmatizing shaming and the prevalence of crime, violence and criminal subcultures.

The second part of the theory seeks to explain why people generally adhere to behavioral norms, turning the traditional "What causes crime?" question upside down. Braithwaite asserts that societies that use "reintegrative shaming" have lower levels of crime and violence. Reintegrative shaming involves encouraging wrongdoers to experience shame for their actions while allowing them to maintain their dignity. This is accomplished by holding wrongdoers accountable for their actions and providing them with an opportunity to make things right. Conferencing is designed to facilitate a process of reintegrative shaming.

Restorative Justice

Although developed independently from the restorative justice movement, conferencing is considered an important new development in restorative justice practice. Restorative justice views crime, not primarily as a violation of law, but as an offense against people and relationships. Restorative justice identifies three main stakeholders in crime: victim, offender and community. According to the philosophy, the community (however vaguely defined) has a responsibility in facilitating a restorative response to wrongdoing; that response should include holding offenders accountable for their actions and requiring them to make reparation to the victim and the community. Punishment and "just deserts" are not goals of restorative justice, and are viewed as ineffective, undesirable and counterproductive responses to crime (McCold, 1995).

Victim-offender mediation, restitution and community service programs have traditionally been central practices for restorative justice advocates. With the advent of family group conferencing and sentencing circles, the restorative justice movement has recognized the importance of including the personal communities of care of both offenders and victims in the resolution of criminal conflict (Umbreit & Zehr, 1996). Restorative justice practice is moving from excluding the micro-community under early victim-offender mediation models to including them as a central part of the restorative process (Van Ness and Strong, 1997; Wright, 1996).

Tony Marshall (1994) suggests that restorative justice seeks to reduce crime by strengthening bonds of interdependency while holding offenders accountable. Marshall defines restorative justice as:

> a process whereby all the parties with a stake in a particular offence come together to resolve collectively how to deal with the aftermath of the offence and its implications for the future. Parties with a stake in an offence include, of course, the victim and the offender, but they also include the families of each, and any other members of their respective communities who may be affected, or who may be able to contribute to prevention of a reoccurrence. (Marshall in McCold, 1997b, p.2)

Restorative Policing

Police-based family group conferencing exemplifies a union of community and problem-oriented policing (especially as conceived by Goldstein), reintegrative shaming and restorative justice—a union which could be termed "restorative policing" (McCold and Wachtel, 1998). As an operational philosophy for police, restorative policing seeks to:
1) Encourage accountability, reparation, reintegration and healing.
2) Reduce recidivism.
3) Resolve conflict and eliminate ongoing problems.
4) Provide communities with a satisfying experience of justice.
5) Reduce reliance on the criminal justice system and formal processes.
6) Transform police attitudes, organizational culture and role perceptions.

Some have expressed concerns and criticisms about police-based family group conferencing, which could be extended to restorative policing as a whole. Efforts to institute restorative policing programs such as conferencing should consider these as part of their evaluation. These concerns and criticisms include:

1) The focus on improving criminal justice responses distracts from the broader goal of tackling social injustice.
2) Conferencing may lead to net-widening.
3) Conferencing threatens principles of proportionality; that is, outcomes from conferencing may be too severe or too lenient compared to outcomes from formal justice processes.
4) Conferencing poses a risk of double jeopardy,
5) Conferencing coerces offenders to admit guilt and threatens due process.

6) Police should not run conferences because they "have a coercive role, their legitimacy is grounded in the invocation of punishment and they do not enjoy the respect of young people, especially young people from oppressed racial groups. So, it is argued, it is naive to believe the police could do a good job." (Braithwaite, 1994, p.207).

Proponents of victim-offender mediation have articulated a number of possible dangers of police-based conferencing, similar to the concerns articulated above (Umbreit and Zehr, 1996):

1) Inadequate preparation could "significantly limit the impact of FGC in humanizing the process in such a manner that parties feel safe and prepared to attend and participate freely in a genuine dialogue" (p.6).
2) Conferencing and conference facilitators may be insensitive to victims' needs and coercive in encouraging their participation in the process.
3) Young offenders may be intimidated by adults and uniformed police officers; they may not feel safe or comfortable enough to share thoughts and feelings and to genuinely "own up" to the criminal behavior.
4) Police may be incapable of being neutral facilitators, falling into authoritarian behavior patterns and undermining the process of reintegrative shaming.
5) The scripted conferencing process may be too rigid and insensitive to cultural needs and preferences within a community.
6) Police-based conferencing may lead to net-widening.

Developing Hypotheses

The only completed empirical evaluation of restorative policing to date is a study of the program in Wagga Wagga, which used a before/after design (Moore, 1995). The "Wagga report" concluded that implementation of conferencing for juvenile offenders had decreased the number of cases being dealt with by formal processing in the court without increasing the overall recidivism rate. The introduction of FGC provided the police with an additional informal process beyond counsel and release, and changed the manner that police disposed of youthful offenders. The rate of referral to court was reduced from 51 percent to 28 percent following the introduction of conferencing. The results also suggested that the introduction of FGC was truly diversionary, without producing a net-widening effect.

The program in Wagga Wagga received widespread support from frontline police personnel and local community members (Graham, 1993; Moore, 1995, 1993; Moore and McDonald, 1995; Moore and O'Connell, 1994). The initial evaluation of the approach demonstrated that juveniles were able to be diverted from formal court processing without increasing the rate of recidivism. Crime victims found overwhelming satisfaction by being actively involved in the process, and families were supported in their efforts to deal with the misbehavior of their children. Victim participation exceeded 90 percent, mutually accepted restitution agreements were developed in 95 percent of conferenced cases, and offenders complied with these agreements more than 95 percent of the time. The active involvement of the community in resolving juvenile crime altered both the view of police toward the community and young people, and the community's view of the police (Moore, 1995).

Moore's study had a number of inherent weaknesses. Due to the lack of a randomized design, the group of offenders processed before the introduction of FGC were not strictly comparable to those processed after its introduction. Rates of re-apprehension were somewhat higher for those processed by the courts following introduction of FGC, and appeared to have remained unchanged for those processed informally by the police (warning versus conferencing). This suggests that re-offending was more a function of choice of processing than the effects of the conferencing, per se.

The few qualitative studies of the Wagga Wagga program have suggested that one of the most significant effects of conferencing was on the attitude that the police department had toward itself. These studies suggest that involvement by the police in conferencing produced a cultural shift from a punitive legalistic approach to a more problem-solving, restorative approach. Additionally, ". . .when police are involved with this more complex model [conferencing], they find it far more satisfying than the traditional alternative" (Moore, 1995, p.212).

John Braithwaite, Lawrence Sherman and Heather Strang are currently collaborating in the Reintegrative Shaming Experiment (RISE) in Canberra, Australia (Sherman, 1996; Sherman and Barnes, 1997; Sherman and Strang, 1997a, 1997b; Strang, 1997; Strang, H. & Sherman, 1997). The RISE project is randomly assigning juvenile offenders and adult "drink driving" offenders to police-run "community accountability conferences" or to traditional court. They are conducting in-depth evaluations of participants' perceptions, victim and offender background information, and systematically observing both the conferences and the court processes. The results of RISE will be an important supplement to the present study and should allow for a cross-national comparison of police-based conferencing.

The primary purpose of the present study is to evaluate the implementation of conferencing as a restorative policing practice, examining the effects of the practice on police and the community and comparing those results to equivalent data on formal adjudication and other restorative justice approaches. Reflecting the goals of restorative policing and the concerns about police-based conferencing previously described, the present study asks the following questions:

1. Can typical American police officers conduct conferences consistent with due process and restorative justice principles?
2. Does conferencing transform police attitudes, organizational culture and role perceptions?
3. Does conferencing produce conflict-reducing outcomes by helping to solve ongoing problems and reduce recidivism?
4. Will victims, offenders and the community accept a police-based restorative justice response?
5. How does the introduction of conferencing alter the case processing of juvenile offenders?
6. How does conferencing compare to the existing system and to other restorative justice programs?

Chapter 2 describes the Bethlehem Police Family Group Conferencing Project in detail. Chapters 3 through 8 examine the present research in light of these six questions. The final chapter draws together the conclusions from the other chapters to address what can be known about these questions from the present findings.

2

The Bethlehem Experiment

In the summer of 1995, the Bethlehem Police Department and the Community Service Foundation (a private not-for-profit organization) began planning a two-year research partnership to study the effectiveness of police-based family group conferencing. Sponsored by the National Institute of Justice*, the study began November 1, 1995, after a three-day REAL JUSTICE® training for 18 Bethlehem Police officers, conducted by three Australian pioneers in family group conferencing.

The Bethlehem Police Department has 140 sworn police officers and is actively involved in addressing the needs of city residents. The department has ongoing crime prevention and community policing programs which include four permanent substations, a mobile substation, bicycle patrols, and four full-time officers assigned to middle schools.

The city of Bethlehem is located in southeastern Pennsylvania, a two-hour drive west of New York City and a one-and-a-half hour drive north of Philadelphia. Bethlehem, Allentown and Easton comprise a three-city metropolitan area, surrounded by approximately 25 townships and boroughs of varying sizes. Bethlehem has an area slightly over 19 square miles with a population of approximately 72,000. It is part of both Northampton and Lehigh counties.

Before the experiment began, the department began a vigorous marketing effort to gain the community's support for the diversion program, which included presentations to service organizations, merchant associations, school administrators and church groups. Several articles appeared in the local newspapers.

Over the course of the experiment, the 18 police officers participating in the program had quarterly meetings to review the progress of the program, identify and resolve problems and be appraised of current research statistics. The group operated as a self-directed work team with a senior officer as liaison (program liaison officer) between the department, courts, probation and schools. The group formulated a program name, "Operation P.R.O.J.E.C.T." (Program for Redirection of Offending Juveniles through Empathy-building and Conferencing Techniques), and developed a mission statement and goals for the program. The mission statement reads:

> The Bethlehem Police Department's "Operation P.R.O.J.E.C.T." is an alternative justice program for juvenile offenders and their victims. By providing a forum for victims to express feeling and take part in the repair of harm, the offenders must own and evaluate their behavior and how it affects other people.

The program goals the officers articulated were satisfying victims, repairing harm/damage, re-educating juvenile offenders, offenders "owning" their behavior, lowering recidi-

---

*This project was supported under award number 95-IJ-CX-0042 from the National Institute of Justice, Office of Justice Programs, U.S. Department of Justice. Points of view in this document are those of the authors and do not necessarily represent the official position of the U.S. Department of Justice.

vism rates, providing an alternative to punishment, increasing community satisfaction, and reducing court system workload.

The following section describes the methods used for selecting cases for the study and soliciting participation in the program. A presentation and discussion of case selection results and participation rates follows.

Methods

The Bethlehem Police Department adopted the following policy for eligibility in the juvenile diversion program:

> - Only juveniles arrested by the Bethlehem Police Department are eligible.*
> - Only first-time offenders are eligible. (For the purpose of the research project, a first-time offender is defined as a juvenile who has not been through the juvenile probation system.)
> - No felony level crimes are eligible unless specifically agreed to by the chief of juvenile probation.
> - No drug or alcohol crimes (possession or delivery) are eligible.
> - No sex offenses are eligible.
> - Only assaults which meet the following conditions are eligible:
>   a) graded as simple assaults (or threat or harassment) where:
>   1) there is no serious bodily injury
>   2) no weapons were used
>   3) juvenile assaults a juvenile where there is less than a 5- year age gap
>   b) graded as a summary violation
> - Thefts of a misdemeanor or summary level are eligible.
> - Property crimes of a misdemeanor or summary level are eligible.

The above policy and guidelines were established after conferring with the juvenile court judges, district attorneys, and chief juvenile probation officers from both Lehigh and Northampton counties. Because this was a pilot program, the cases selected for inclusion were confined to the least serious cases available. A limited number of prior summary arrests did not automatically disqualify a juvenile from the program, allowing for some discretion by the program liaison officer, in consultation with the principal investigator. Cases where the only identifiable victim was the arresting officer—so-called "contempt of cop" cases—were not included in the study, at the request of the principal investigator.

The program liaison officer regularly reviewed arrest records submitted by officers over the course of the experiment—November 1, 1995 through May 1, 1997—earmarking cases that appeared to qualify for the study. Criminal history information was then checked to confirm eligibility. The liaison officer then phoned the principal investigator to submit the selected cases to random assignment.

There were to be a total of 150 crime-against-property cases and 75 crime-against-

---

* As of October 1996, this requirement was amended with the Hellertown Police Department joining the project. Hellertown is a smaller jurisdiction adjacent to Bethlehem. The Hellertown Police contributed one case to the experiment.

person cases selected for the experiment, two-thirds assigned to a treatment group and one-third assigned to a control group. Cases were defined as a criminal incident, and each case could involve multiple offenders.

Two lists of random numbers had been generated ($n = 150$ and $n = 75$), each with equal distributions of integers 1, 2 and 3. The cases were placed on a list in the order they were reported to the researcher. All incidents with 1's were coded as the control group, 2's and 3's the treatment group. The random assignment list was never revealed to the liaison officer, and he could not anticipate the next assignment. When a case was included, a determination was made whether the offense was primarily a crime-against-property or primarily a crime-against-person, hereafter referred to as property crimes and violent crimes. The case information was then entered into the next line of the relevant random list and the liaison officer was informed whether the case was control or treatment.

None of the victims or offenders for control group cases were informed about the existence of the diversion program. These cases were left to be processed without police diversion. When a case was assigned to the treatment group, the liaison officer began to attempt to contact the offender(s) involved, explain the program and elicit their participation. Because the program is mindful of the due process rights of offenders, they must understand that they can opt out of the program and decide to face court with all their rights intact. Acceptance into the program required the offender to admit non-inculpatory responsibility for the charge (actus reus). When offenders agreed to participate, the liaison officer then contacted the victims to explain the program and elicit their participation. Only where both offender and victim were willing to participate was the case assigned to the facilitating officer. If either party was unwilling to participate, the case was not conferenced and, thus, was processed through normal channels like the control cases. After the key parties agreed to participate, the facilitating officer then had the responsibility of inviting other supporters, arranging a time and place to meet, and speaking with all participants to prepare them for the conference.

Results

There were 1,285 juveniles arrests between November 1, 1995, and May 1, 1997 (excluding traffic violations). As reflected in the selection criteria above, the Bethlehem Police Department wanted to exclude repeat offenders, offenders charged with felony offenses, and those not residing locally; the county prosecutors wanted to exclude drug and alcohol offenses, sex offenses, weapon offenses, and assaults where offenders used a weapon or were more than four years apart in age from the victim; the principal investigator wanted to avoid crimes where the only available victim was the arresting officer and cases disposed without formal arrest. These are not mutually exclusive categories. For example, 56 percent of the offenders charged with a felony were also disqualified

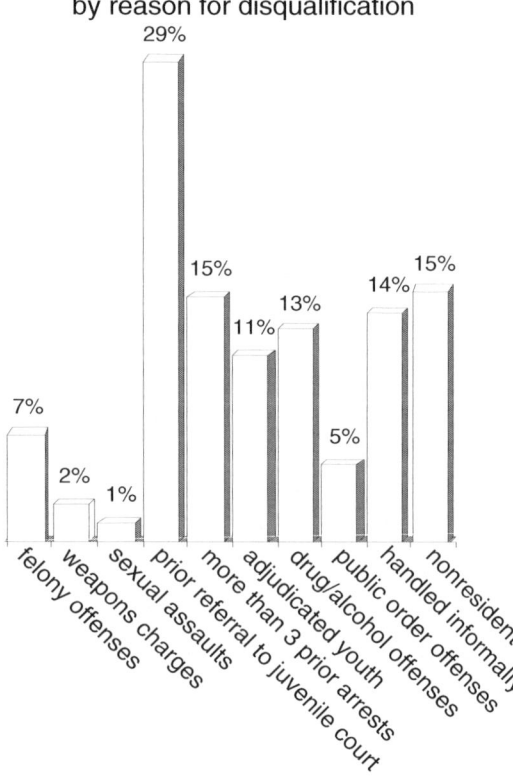

Exhibit 1
Proportion of total juvenile arrests disqualified from study by reason for disqualification

because of prior records.

As shown in Exhibit 1, prior referral to juvenile probation (i.e., prior misdemeanor or felony arrest) was the largest single reason for disqualifying cases from the study, with 29 percent who could have been disqualified for that reason alone. Overall, 35 percent of offenders could have been disqualified for one or more of the three prior history reasons (prior referral to juvenile court, more than 3 prior arrests or adjudicated youth), 18 percent for inappropriate crimes (drug and alcohol or public order offenses), 15 percent for non-Bethlehem-residency, 14 percent for too trivial an offense (handled informally), and 10 percent for too serious a crime (felony, weapons or sexual offenses).

There were 227 juvenile arrests during the study—18 percent of the total number of arrests ($n = 1,285$)—who could not be disqualified based on any of the known reasons stated above. Some of these cases were not selected because of offenders who were charged with a simple assault in spite of using a weapon or who had committed disorderly conduct without a victim other than the arresting officer. This detailed information was only available from the arrest reports, and thus these offenders could not be disqualified based upon information available from the computerized records. Nonetheless, this apparently qualifying but not selected group of offenders will provide a useful comparison group later in this report.

In order to compare the proportions of cases disqualified for different reasons, it is necessary to create mutually exclusive categories. If cases are first disqualified because the crime was too serious, then because the offender's prior history was too serious, then because the offenses were inappropriate, then because the case was handled informally, and finally because the offender was not a local resident, an approximation of proportions of cases disqualified by reason can be considered.

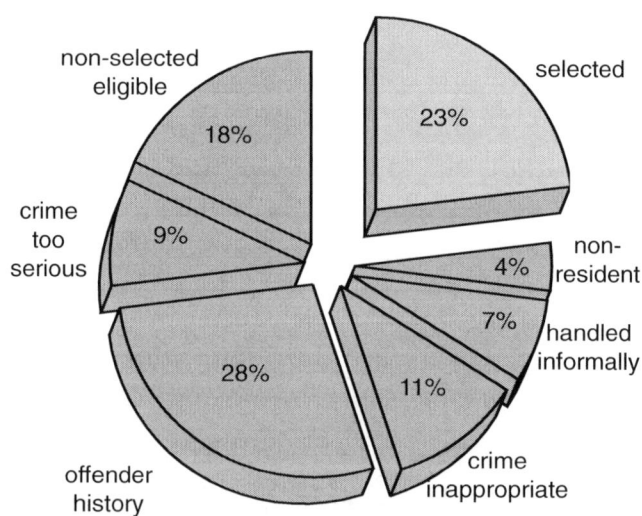

Exhibit 2
Offender eligibility categories
n = 1,285

As shown in Exhibit 2, offender prior history remains the most common disqualifier (28 percent), followed by inappropriate offenses (11 percent) and crime seriousness (9 percent). Eighteen percent of all juvenile arrests were disqualified for reasons not available in computerized records. Thus, during the course of the experiment, 215 criminal incidents involving the arrests of 292 juveniles qualified for the study, representing 23 percent of all juvenile offenders arrested by the Bethlehem Police during the time period.

Qualifying cases were submitted to random assignment until the target rate of 75 violent crimes was achieved. The project included 140 property crimes, 93 percent of the 150-case target. The results of the random assignment are shown in Exhibit 3. The randomized experimental assignment was adhered to in all 215 cases in the study, achieving the one-third/two-thirds assignment with less than .24 percent deviation. The number of offenders per case ranged from 1 to 6, with an overall average of 1.36 persons-per-crime (ppc). This ratio did not distribute equally across the experimental groups. Among violent cases, treatment and control groups were about equally as likely to involve multiple offenders with 1.40 ppc in the control group and 1.52 ppc in the treatment group. However, among property cases, the treatment group, with 1.22 ppc, was less likely to involve multiple offenders than the control group, with 1.45 ppc. Thus, treatment group property cases were less likely to have involved multiple offenders than cases in the other groups. As a result, the assignment of offenders slightly deviates from the case distribution as shown in Exhibit 4, though not by a statistically significant amount.

Exhibit 3
Random assignment results - Cases

	total		control		treatment	
violent	75	100%	25	33%	50	67%
property	140	100%	47	34%	93	66%
column	215	100%	72	33%	143	67%

Exhibit 4
Random assignment results - Offenders

	total		control		treatment	
violent	111	100%	35	32%	76	68%
property	181	100%	68	38%	113	62%
column	292	100%	103	35%	189	65%

The participation rates in the program for those cases assigned to be conferenced (treatment group) varied, with 32 percent of violent cases and 52 percent of property cases participating. Taking into account that there were multiple offenders for some cases, the offender-based participation rates were slightly lower, with 32 percent of violent offenders and 50 percent of property offenders participating, as shown in Exhibit 5. Thus, two-thirds of the violent offenders and half of the property offenders selected for experimental treatment were actually processed the same as those selected for the control group, through the traditional court processes, χ^2 (1, n = 189) = 6.06, p < .05.

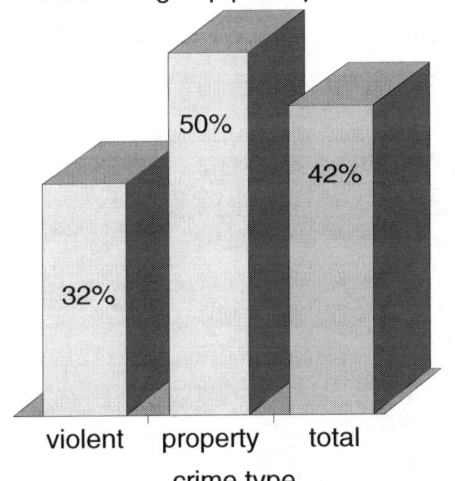

Exhibit 5
Treatment group participation rates

It was expected that the randomly assigned groups

would be similar in all important respects. Because a proportion of those cases selected for treatment failed to result in a conference, the assumption of equality of groups is in doubt. Thus, there are essentially three experimental groups—the control group, the conference group (treatment/participation) and the decline group (treatment/non-participation). Knowledge of any ways the groups differ will be helpful in interpreting results from this study.

Exhibit 6
Arrest charges for offenders included in study by experimental group

	total		control		conference		decline	
retail theft	129	44%	44	43%	48	60%	37	34%
criminal mischief	24	8%	7	7%	6	8%	11	10%
theft by unlawful taking	10	3%	4	4%	1	1%	5	5%
receiving stolen property	4	1%	1	1%			3	3%
criminal trespass	4	1%	4	4%				
disorderly conduct	4	1%	4	4%				
park after hours	2	1%	2	2%				
theft/failure to deposit	1	0%			1	1%		
institutional vandalism	1	0%	1	1%				
false alarm	1	0%	1	1%				
unauth.use of vehicle	1	0%					1	1%
Property Subtotal	181	62%	68	66%	56	70%	57	52%
disorderly conduct	49	18%	18	21%	10	13%	21	19%
harassment	38	13%	12	12%	6	8%	20	18%
simple assault	20	7%	2	2%	7	9%	11	10%
terroristic threats	2	1%	2	2%				
harass.by communication	1	0%	1	1%				
noise a nuisance	1	0%			1	1%		
Violent Subtotal	111	38%	35	34%	24	30%	52	48%
Total	292	100%	103	100%	80	100%	109	100%

The specific criminal offenses included in the sample are shown in Exhibit 6. Among property crimes, 74 percent were retail theft cases. Among the violent crimes, 88 percent were harassment or disorderly conduct. Harassment-by-communication is included in the harassment category, and all other crimes are collapsed to produce the specific crime groupings used in this study. Thus, property crimes are divided into retail theft and other property crimes, and violent offenders are divided into three crime types—disorderly, harassment and other violent crimes—as shown in Exhibit 7.

Among property crimes, retail theft cases were somewhat under-represented in the control group and over-represented in the conference group. Participation rates were

Exhibit 7
Arrest charge categories for offenders included in study by experimental group

	total		control		conference		decline	
retail theft	129	71%	44	65%	48	86%	37	65%
other theft	52	29%	24	35%	8	14%	20	35%
Property Subtotal	181	100%	68	100%	56	100%	57	100%
disorderly conduct	49	18%	18	21%	10	13%	21	19%
harassment	38	13%	12	12%	6	8%	20	18%
other violent	25	23%	6	17%	8	33%	11	21%
Violent Subtotal	111	100%	35	39%	24	30%	52	48%
Total	292	100%	103	100%	80	100%	109	100%

58 percent for retail theft and 29 percent for other property crimes. Among violent offenders, the crime subcategories are more equally distributed across all three experimental groups, and the participation rates were comparable, with 35 percent for disorderly, 32 percent for harassment, and 40 percent for other violent crimes. Thus, the only difference in the distribution of crime subcategories across experimental groups was that among property offenders those offenders attending a conference were more likely to be charged with retail theft versus other property crimes than those offenders in the control or decline groups.

Exhibit 8 shows the experimental groups broken down by age, seriousness of charge, race/ethnicity, gender and residence. Differences between experimental groups in seriousness of charge and race/ethnicity are not statistically significant controlling for crime type. However, differences in age, gender and residence are statistically significant after controlling for crime type. Thus, the experimental groups differed in several respects. Among violent offenders, males comprised half the conference group and 75 percent of the decline group. Among property offenders, the decline group had a lower proportion of 13-year-olds and a higher proportion of Zip1 residents than the conference and decline groups; the property control group had a higher proportion of Zip3 residents than the property decline and

Exhibit 8
Experimental Group Comparisons

	Total			Violent			Property		
	control	conference	decline	control	conference	decline	control	conference	decline
number	103	80	109	35	24	52	68	56	57
Age on arrest									
under13	25%	23%	24%	14%	21%	19%	31%	23%	28%
age13	29%	29%	16%	29%	38%	23%	29%	25%	9%
age14-15	34%	31%	32%	46%	21%	25%	28%	36%	39%
age16-17	12%	18%	28%	11%	21%	33%	12%	16%	25%
χ^2,p	13.2	0.04		9.7	ns		11.4	0.08	
Most serious current arrest									
summary	89%	98%	93%	86%	96%	87%	91%	98%	98%
misdemr-3	5%	0%	0%	3%	0%	0%	6%	0%	0%
misdemr-2	3%	3%	7%	6%	4%	13%	1%	2%	2%
felony-2	2%	0%	0%	6%	0%	0%	0%	0%	0%
χ^2,p	18.3	0.02		8.9	ns		8.6	ns	
Race/Ethnicity									
white	44%	41%	35%	37%	29%	31%	47%	46%	39%
black	6%	1%	14%	6%	0%	13%	6%	2%	14%
Latino	49%	51%	50%	57%	63%	54%	44%	46%	46%
other	2%	6%	2%	0%	8%	2%	3%	5%	2%
χ^2,p	15.0	0.02		8.5	ns		7.9	ns	
Gender									
male	71%	53%	69%	83%	50%	75%	65%	54%	63%
female	29%	48%	31%	17%	50%	25%	35%	46%	37%
χ^2,p	7.8	0.02		8.1	0.02		1.8	ns	
Number of current charges									
one	88%	94%	82%	91%	96%	81%	87%	93%	82%
two	9%	5%	14%	9%	4%	10%	9%	5%	18%
>two	3%	1%	5%	0%	0%	10%	4%	2%	0%
χ^2,p	6.3	ns		6.8	ns		7.4	ns	
Number of prior arrests									
none	78%	83%	75%	69%	63%	65%	82%	91%	84%
one	17%	15%	17%	23%	29%	25%	13%	9%	11%
two	6%	0%	6%	9%	0%	8%	4%	0%	5%
>two	0%	3%	1%	0%	8%	2%	0%	0%	0%
χ^2,p	6.3	ns		6.8	ns		7.4	ns	
Residence of offender									
Zip1	28%	33%	48%	31%	38%	50%	26%	30%	46%
Zip2	33%	36%	34%	37%	38%	31%	31%	36%	37%
Zip3	36%	20%	13%	29%	17%	13%	40%	21%	12%
Other	3%	11%	6%	3%	8%	6%	3%	13%	5%
χ^2,p	24.1	0.00		5.6	ns		18.2	0.01	

conference groups. There was no discernable differences in the three Zip codes which might explain these differences in participation by locality (residents differed as much within zip code as between zip codes in S.E.S. and racial composition). In all other respects, based on the available data, the decline group is statistically similar to the conference group, and the control group is statistically similar to the conference and decline groups.

Understanding the reasons for declining to participate may help expose a self-selection bias should one exist. Because conferencing is voluntary, either victim or offender could decline to participate. Other factors besides direct refusals to participate could also result in failure of conferences to proceed. Cases were coded by the reason for declining to participate as shown in Exhibit 9a.

Exhibit 9a
Reasons for cases declining to participate

	total		violent		property	
offender declined	55	50%	15	29%	40	70%
contests charges	12		5		7	
prefers court	20		6		14	
reoffend prior to contact	6		1		5	
unable to contact	17		3		14	
victim declined	40	37%	32	62%	8	14%
victim declined	22		14		8	
victim nonresponsive	18		18		0	
case excluded	14	13%	5	10%	9	16%
settled prior to contact	9		4		5	
administrative error	5		1		4	
column	109		52		57	

Among the 52 selected violent offenders not conferenced, offenders declined in 29 percent of the cases and the victim declined in 62 percent of the cases. Among the 57 selected property offenders not conferenced, the corresponding decline proportions were 70 percent for offenders, and 14 percent for victims. Thus, offenders were much more likely to be the reason for declining conferencing in property offenses, victims more likely in violent offenses.

The program participation rate is the number of conferences divided by the number of cases selected in the treatment group. In order to calculate individual victim and offender participation rates, it is necesary to limit the categories in the denominator of the rate. For example, offenders who could not be found could not have agreed or declined to participate, so they should not be counted in the offender decline figure. Likewise, victims of offenders who declined to participate were never ask to participate, so the number of cases for victims to available to decline is limited to the number of conferences (where offender has agreed to participate) plus the number of victims declining.

Exhibit 9b
Corrected participation rates

	total	violent	property	formulas
total selected for treatment	189	76	113	
total cases declined	109	52	57	
excluded cases	14	5	9	
reoffend prior to contact	6	1	5	
offenders unable to contact	17	3	14	
offender decline	32	11	21	
victim decline	40	32	8	
conferenced	80	24	56	
offender participate rate	79%	84%	75%	=(vic+conf)/(off+vic+conf)
victim participate rate	67%	43%	88%	=(conf)/(vic+conf)
total participation rate	53%	36%	66%	=conf/(off+vic+conf)
program participation rate	42%	32%	50%	=conf/total selected

Exhibit 10a
Participation rates of treatment-selected offenders

	total		violent		property	
	%partic	cases	%partic	cases	%partic	cases
total	42%	189	32%	76	50%	113
age on arrest						
<13	41%	44	33%	15	45%	29
13	58%	40	43%	21	74%	19
14-15	42%	60	28%	18	48%	42
16-17	31%	45	23%	22	39%	23
χ^2,p	6.1	ns	2.2	ns	5.7	ns
most serious current charge						
summary	44%	179	34%	68	50%	111
misdemr	20%	10	13%	8	50%	2
χ^2,p	2.2	ns	1.5	ns	0.0	ns
race/ethnicity						
white	46%	71	30%	23	54%	48
black	6%	16	0%	7	11%	9
Latino	43%	95	35%	43	50%	52
other	71%	7	67%	3	75%	4
χ^2,p	11.5	.01	5.2	ns	6.8	ns
gender						
male	36%	117	24%	51	45%	66
female	53%	72	48%	25	55%	47
χ^2,p	5.2	.02	4.6	.03	1.1	ns

The formulas for computing individual victim and offender participation rates is shown in Exhibit 9b. Offenders agreed to participated 79% of the times they were asked (85% violent and 75% property). Victims agreed to participate 67% of the times they were asked (43% violent; 88% property). When offered a conference victims and offenders agreed to participate 53% of the time (36% violent; 66% property). Thus the program participation rate of 42% (and 32% and 50%, respectively) underestimate the true participation rate.

Part of the reason for crime-specific differences in participation rates relates to the type of victim for each offense. Institutions were the victims in 61 percent of the cases included in this study. A store was the victim in 76 percent of all property cases ($n = 140$). The school was the victim in 29 percent of violent cases ($n = 75$). Although the local schools did participate in the program, the number of cases occurring at one local high school created scheduling problems for the school administrators. A number of cases were excluded from the diversion program because the schools were unresponsive in scheduling a time for the conference to occur.

Participation rates also differed by race and gender and, to a lesser extent by seriousness and number of current charges, as shown in Exhibit 10a and Exhibit 10b. However, when type of crime is controlled for, the only difference which remains significant is gender, with females participating at twice the rate as males for violent cases. The differences in participation rates by race/ethnicity and number of current charges are due to differing proportions of these cases by crime type. There was a tendency for those charged with more serious offenses and a greater number of offenses to decline participation at higher rates than others, though these differences are not statistically significant given the number of cases.

Exhibit 10b
Participation rates of treatment-selected offenders (continued)

	total		violent		property	
	%partic	cases	%partic	cases	%partic	cases
number of current charges						
one	46%	164	35%	65	53%	99
two	21%	19	17%	6	23%	13
>two	17%	6	0%	5	100%	1
χ^2,p	5.9	ns	3.4	ns	5.0	ns
number of prior arrests						
none	45%	148	31%	49	52%	99
one	39%	31	35%	20	45%	11
two	0%	7	0%	4	0%	3
>two	67%	3	67%	3		
χ^2,p	6.3	ns	3.7	ns	3.2	ns
residence						
zip1	33%	78	26%	35	40%	43
zip2	44%	66	36%	25	49%	41
zip3	53%	30	36%	11	63%	19
other	60%	15	40%	5	70%	10
χ^2,p	6.1	ns	1.1	ns	4.8	ns

Exhibit 11
Offender case disposition by crime type and court group

	total		violent		property	
	control	decline	control	decline	control	decline
%convict	66%	54%	59%	51%	70%	57%
informal	28	34	12	17	16	17
acquit	5	8	2	4	3	4
convict	65	50	20	22	45	28
column	98	92	34	43	64	49

Exhibit 12
Magistrate findings for cases in study disposed by magistrate court

	violent			property		
	control	decline	subtotal	control	decline	subtotal
%plea	55%	68%	61%	93%	74%	87%
χ^2,p	0.3	ns		4.5	.03	
%dismiss	21%	21%	21%	19%	23%	20%
χ^2,p	0.8	ns		0.0	ns	
Number of Cases						
guilty plea	12	12	24	37	16	53
accelerated disp.		3	3	4	1	5
guilty trial	8	2	10		2	2
not guilty	2	5	7	3	4	7
withdrawn		1	1	2	1	3
dismissed	6	5	11	8	6	14
no finding	7	24	31	14	27	41
column	35	52	87	68	57	125

A question remains about the differences between the control groups and the decline groups. The degree to which the cases are different in legally relevant ways (e.g., crime seriousness, prior record) should be reflected in the court disposition of these cases. However, as shown in Exhibit 11, only the control property cases had a greater chance of conviction, though this difference was not statistically significant. Thus, there is some reason to think that the property control group is different in relevant ways from the other court processed cases (violent control group and the violent and property decline groups).

Considering the disposition of all the court cases in the study, as shown in Exhibit 12, there were no statistically significant difference in the proportion of cases dismissed (withdrawn or dismissed) or in guilty plea rates except among the property cases: 93 percent of the formally disposed property control cases pled guilty (plea or accelerated disposition) compared to 74 percent of the property decline cases.

Conclusions

The random assignment of violent offenders produced similar groups, alike in all measured respects; this was not true for the random assignment of property offenders. In spite of adhering to a strict random assignment, the control group of property offenders differed in a number of respects from the treatment group of property offenders. This control group was more likely to include multiple offenders per case compared to the conference group or the decline group. Also, the property control group was much more likely than either the conference or decline groups to reside in the Zip1 area of Bethlehem. Finally, the control group of property offenders were more likely to have pled guilty than other cases in the study disposed by court to date.

Property offenders were more likely to participate in a conference, with half the property offenders participating in a conference, compared to only a third of the violent offenders. This great of a non-participation rate has serious implications for the internal validity of the experiment, making program effects indistinguishable from the effects of having the more cooperative cases. The empirical evicence of a pure program effect will have to await the results of the RISE project (Sherman, 1996). Since cases in RISE are randomly assigned to treatment only after offenders have agreed to participate, presumably their entire sample is a subset of our sample. Excluded from the RISE sample are those offenders who themselves decline to participate in addition to those cases not qualifying. Thus, as in any truly voluntary program, self-selection bias in the sample is unavoidable. This bias will have greater effect for the internal validity of the present study and for the external validity of the RISE study.

In spite of the potential self-selection bias in the treatment group, much can be learned about implementation from the external validity (generalizability) of the sample which was maintained. For this experiment to demonstrate a "program effect" and differences in outcomes to reach statistical significance, the program effects would have to be strong enough to be measured across the entire treatment-selected group, even though less than half received the treatment. Presumably, the decline groups received the same treatment conditions as their respective control groups, so the program effects should be independent of the self-selection effect, only substantially watered-down by the low participation rate. Thus, only differences between control group and combined treatment group (conference and decline) are tests of pure program effects apart from self-selection effects.

Questions about how police conducted conferences, whether this affected their culture, whether the community will accept the program, and how the program affected case processing do not require equilivant comparison groups and are unaffected by the lack of internal validiy of the random assignment (also see the discussion on limitations in the final chapter below).

3
Conference Observations

In October 1995, the Bethlehem Police Department was in the process of integrating community and problem-oriented policing over the entire department. Family group conferencing showed obvious potential for problem solving. The department sent 18 Bethlehem police officers to a three-day training by several of the Australian innovators of police-based conferencing. Two officers had received similar training six months earlier. The officers who had volunteered were enthusiastic about this new approach.

This training was one of a series of large trainings conducted by the Australians and arranged by REAL JUSTICE, a not-for-profit training organization in Bethlehem, Pennsylvania. These large trainings (60 to 80 police, probation and school officials) were necessary to support the cost of transporting the Australians to the U.S. REAL JUSTICE has since evolved the training model as a U.S.- and Canada-based organization and limits training size, often conducting trainings for as few as 15 people at a time. The three-day training seemed to be insufficient in providing the officers with proper personal attention and rationale for doing the new process. Nonetheless, the trained officers and the department recognized the problem-solving potential in the process and proceeded enthusiastically.

Once every trained officer had conducted at least one conference, a one-day meeting was held with the facilitating officers where feedback on their performance evaluations was provided by the police lieutenant in charge of in-service training.[*] There had been a tendency among some officers to be unprepared for the conferences, meeting many of the participants for the first time at the conference, straying from or paraphrasing the conference script, and in two cases, deciding for the group that the offender should perform community service. Shaming offenders in a stigmatizing manner is antithetical to restorative policing, which should involve reintegrative shaming. Yet, in spite of the training the officers had received, some seemed surprised that they were not supposed to lecture the offender or affect the conference agreements.

The other criticism was that conferences tended to be too small, without enough supporters for the victims and the offenders, especially other young people and extended family members. The officer with the poorest performance evaluation withdrew from the program and a total of five officers (20 percent) never conferenced a second case. There were 27 conferences involving 34 offenders conducted before this meeting and 37 conducted after involving 46 offenders.

The following is a report on the conference observations and performance evaluations, including an analysis of how various observations relate to each other and to other variables, and a report on conference outcomes.

---

[*] The project's research advisory board recommended taking this corrective action. It was agreed that, because the officers were not conducting conferences according to protocol, such a direct intervention in the program operation was warranted.

Methods

To enhance consistency in evaluations of conference facilitator performance, an observation form was developed (see appendix for complete form). The three observers discussed the observation form, gave each other feedback and practiced using the form with conference role plays from the REAL JUSTICE training until there was reasonable consistency between ratings on the scales. The principal investigator observed and rated 95 percent of all observed conferences. In two cases only the observations of the project researcher were used, and in one case, only the observations of the police liaison officer was used. Scales developed from the combined observers ratings were found to be reliable as described below.

There were three parts to the conference observations. The first was a checklist of seven items that facilitators were supposed to do in every conference. These included:

1) Introducing all participants.
2) Obtaining permission for observers.
3) Acknowledging appreciation of everyone's effort to attend.
4) Setting the conference focus.
5) Telling offenders they had the right to terminate the conference at any time.
6) Checking that offenders understood this right.
7) Making sure offenders took clear responsibility for their behavior as they told their story in the conference.

The second part of conference observation was to watch the conference and observe any of six types of actions, inappropriate and appropriate, that facilitators might do. Observers made a check for each occurrence. These included:

1) Avoidance of emotion (inappropriate)
2) Use of silence (appropriate)
3) Refocus discussion (appropriate)
4) Failure to refocus (inappropriate)
5) Interrupt participant (inappropriate)
6) Redundant question (inappropriate)

The last part was a list of questions about the facilitator, victim, offender and other participants which were completed after the conference. These were each five-point items:

About facilitator
1) Did the officer maintain the distinction between the person and behavior? (deeddoer)
2) Was any reparation suggested by the officer? (suggest)
3) Was the reparation outcome affected by the officer? (affect)
4) Did the officer lecture the offender? (lecture)
5) To what extent did the officer adhere to conference facilitation protocol? (adhere)

About victim
1) Did the victim seem satisfied with the outcome?
2) Did the victim indicate a sense of forgiveness?

About offender
1) Did the offender appear to understand the injury caused to the victim?
2) Did the offender seem to express sincere remorse?
3) Did the offender appear to end with a feeling of pride?

About other participants
1) Did the offender's family volunteer future responsibility for the offender?
2) Did the offender's supporters volunteer future responsibility for the offender?
3) Was there a strong sense of reconciliation (reintegration)?

The relative reintegration of each conference was scored on a five-point scale item evaluating the relative overall punitiveness based on nature of outcome, lack of offender support shown, and the observed social interaction in the aftermath of the conference.

Facilitator performance was rated using the following scales:
1) a count of the number of missing checks in the seven-item checklist (check 0-7)
2) a count of the number of inappropriate actions by the facilitator (inapprop 0-6)
3) each of the five-point ordinal items asking about the facilitator's overall compliance with conference protocol (deeddoer, suggest, affect, lecture, adhere)

An overall grade of performance was calculated by dividing the sum of the items (positively scored) from the 33 possible points. This produces a percentage scale measuring the extent to which officers adhered to protocol (*alpha* = .77). The overall grades ranged from 21 percent to 100 percent (eight conferences had scores of 100 percent). Additionally, the number of participants was used as part of the overall facilitator performance.

Results

Conference Observations

Conferencing began November 1, 1995 and by the end of April 1997, the Bethlehem Police had conducted 64 conferences involving 80 offenders. Among these, 56 conferences were observed by at least one of three trained observers (27 prior to the in-service training and 29 following), including 14 of the 16 violent cases (82 percent) and 42 of the 48 property cases (88 percent). The participating victims were mostly institutional victims—59 percent retailers and 18 percent schools, as shown in Exhibit 13. In these cases, representatives from the businesses and schools—including store managers and owners, security personnel, and school administrators and faculty—attended the conferences. The remaining 23 percent were personal victims.

The conferences lasted an average of 34 minutes (*min* = 10, *max* = 72), and the post-conference contract preparation and social time lasted an average of 10 minutes (*min* = 5, *max* = 25). The retail theft conferences took less time than other types of offenses, lasted an average of 27 minutes while non-retail theft conferences lasted an average of 47 minutes, $F(1, 53) = 37.3$, $p < .001$. There was no other significant difference in length of con-

Exhibit 13
Type of victims

- retailer 59%
- school 18%
- person 23%

ference or social time between crime types or between the period before the in-service training and the period after the in-service training.

Offenders were conferenced an average of 37 days from the day of the offense ($min = 3$, $max = 121$). The average time between crime and conference in the early period was 30 days compared to 43 days in the later period, $F(1, 78) = 4.8$, $p < .05$, with no difference between crime types. The Bethlehem Police Department had originally intended to conference cases within two weeks of the offense. Only 18 percent of conferenced offenders ($n = 80$) were conferenced within two weeks.

There were an average of 6 participants per conference ($min = 3$, $max = 17$). Retail theft conferences were smaller with an average of 5 participants compared to 8 participants for other types of cases, $F(1, 54) = 14.5$, $p < .001$. There was no change in the average number of participants between periods. The arresting officer was a participant in 25 percent of conferences, 14 percent of retail and 47 percent of others, $\chi^2 (1, n = 56) = 7.7$, $p < .01$. Young persons other than the offender (or victim) were present in 35 percent of the conferences. This was consistent across crime type and time period.

Conference protocol requires that the officer follow a scripted process for the conference (McDonald, et al., 1995). The conference script includes three parts: the preamble, the conference phase and the agreement phase. The preamble is designed to set a non-accusing focus and protect the due process rights of the offender. It requires telling offenders that the conference is voluntary and they have the right to have the case processed through court. This is something of a formality because this should have been made clear to offenders since the initial contact. The conference process is a series of open-ended questions asked of the offender, the victim, the victim's supporters, the offender's supporters and the arresting officers, if present. The agreement phase begins by asking the victim, and then all others, what they would like get out of the conference.

Overall, in 5 (9 percent) of the 56 conferences observed, the facilitating officer either failed to introduce the participants or had them introduce themselves. The facilitator got permission for the observers, expressed appreciation, and set the conference focus in all but 4 (5 percent) of the conferences. In all but 6 (10 percent) of the conferences observed, the facilitator explained the offenders' rights and in all but 8 cases (12 percent) the facilitator checked that the offender understood this right. Facilitators did all of these preamble parts of the conference process in 75 percent of the conferences. There were no significant differences in the number of missing preamble items by crime type or by whether the conference was before or after the in-service meeting.

Conference protocol is followed best when the facilitator does not avoid the emotions of participants, but allows space for the expression of appropriate feelings. Should expressions of feeling become inappropriate—for example, if a participant is angrily browbeating the offender—the facilitator should refocus the conference. Failing to do so is a deviation from protocol. Also, facilitators should allow enough space for each participant to express themselves fully and not inappropriately interrupt. Half the facilitators were completely appropriate, 30 percent had one inappropriate behavior, 9 percent had two and 11 percent had 3 or more.

As shown in Exhibit 14, the average number of inappropriate facilitator responses increased for violent cases and decreased for property cases following the in-service meeting, $F(1, 55) = 6.8$, $p < .05$ for interaction effect.

Part of setting the conference focus is to explain that "we are not here to decide whether [offender] is a good or bad person, but to examine who has been affected by his/her inappropriate behavior." Since maintaining the distinction between deed and doer is important—that is, disapproving of the offense, but not disapproving of the offender as a person—facilitators were evaluated on how well they themselves did at maintaining such a distinction. Seventy-nine percent of all conference facilitators maintained the distinction between person and behavior "completely", 14 percent "mostly", 4 percent "somewhat", 4 percent "a little", and 1 percent "not at all". Facilitators were much more likely to maintain the distinction completely after the in-service training, from 63 percent to 93 percent, χ^2 (1, $n = 56$) = 7.5, $p < .01$. As shown in Exhibit 15, there was general improvement in this score following the in-service training in both crime types, $F(1, 54) = 7.9$, $p < .01$, with facilitators of violent cases all scoring a perfect 5 in the later period.

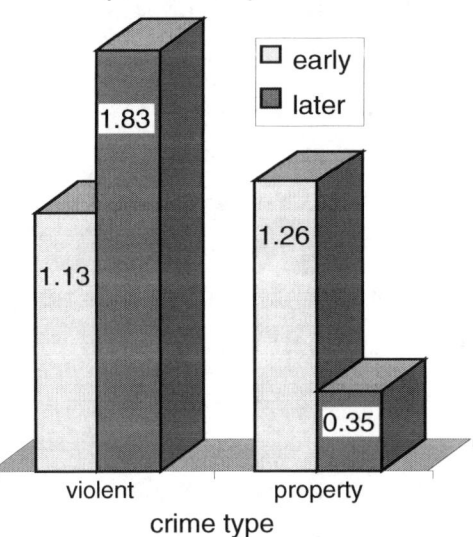

Exhibit 14
Mean number of inappropriate coordinator responses by period of experiment

Conference protocol makes it very clear that the facilitator is not to determine the outcomes of conferences; the outcomes should be an agreement between conference participants. Suggesting or affecting the nature of the agreement is inappropriate for facilitators. Yet, only 59 percent of all facilitators suggested reparation outcomes "not at all", 21 percent "a little", 7 percent "somewhat", 7 percent "mostly", and 5 percent "completely". The proportion not suggesting reparation improved following the in-service training, from 41 percent before to 76 percent after, χ^2 (1, $n = 56$) = 7.1, $p < .01$.

Only 57 percent of all facilitators were scored as not having affected the reparation outcome, 17 percent "a little", 7 percent "somewhat", 14 percent "mostly", and 4 percent "completely". Fifty-five percent of conference facilitators affected the outcome some before the in-service and 31 percent after the in-service, not quite a significant difference, χ^2 (1, n = 56) = 3.4, p = .064. While facilitators of property cases were less likely to suggest or affect the outcome than for violent cases, these differences were not statistically significant.

It was made clear to the facilitating officers that conferencing was not to be just a more formal "counsel and release" process and that it is inappropriate for the facilitator to lecture offenders. Yet only 61 percent of all conference facilitators lectured the offender "not at all", 27 percent "a little", 7 percent "somewhat", 1 percent "mostly", and 4 percent "completely". Fifty-two percent before the in-service and 69 percent after the in-service totally avoided lecturing, though this difference is not significant. Forty-nine percent of retail theft conference facilitators and 21 percent of all other conference facilitators lectured the offender some, χ^2 (1, n = 56) = 4.0, p < .05.

Only 39 percent of all facilitators were scored as having adhered to conference facilitation protocol "completely", 41 percent "mostly", 6 percent "somewhat", and 5 percent "a little". Before the in-service, 70 percent were scored as completely or mostly adhering to protocol, compared to 90 percent after, though this difference was not quite significant, χ^2 (1, n = 56) = 3.3, p = .070.

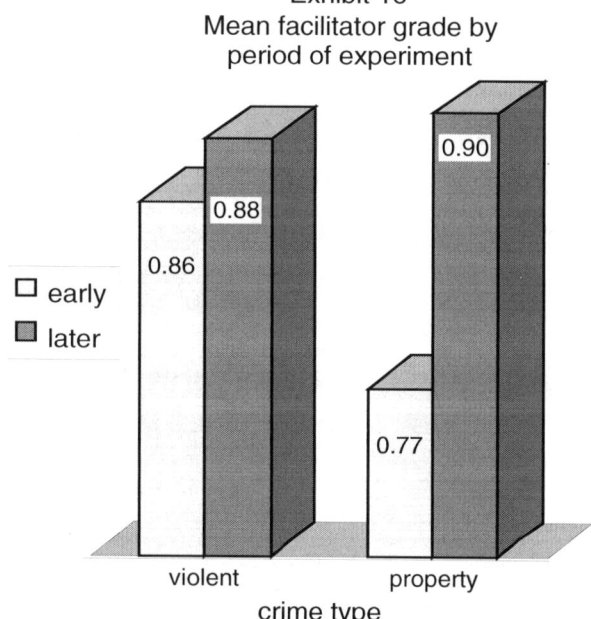

Exhibit 16
Mean facilitator grade by period of experiment

The average grade for facilitator compliance with protocol was 84.7 percent (*median* = 87.9 percent). There was a significant improvement in grades after the in-service, with the average grade increasing from 79.8 percent to 89.3 percent, $F(1, 54)$ = 6.4, p < .05. As shown in Exhibit 16, the greatest improvement in grade was for property offenses, $F(1, 54)$ = 7.0, p < .05.

It appears that facilitators of retail theft conferences were more likely to lecture the offender (65 percent) than facilitators of other types of conferences (20 percent), at least during the early period, χ^2 (1, n = 56) = 5.0, p < .05. There was not a significant overall reduction in the use of lecturing, and the relationship between lecturing and crime type became insignificant after the in-service training (non-retail 22 percent and retail 35 percent).

There were dramatic improvements in overall scores and subscale scores following the in-service training. Scores improved for making introductions, getting permission for observers, expressing appreciation of attendance and setting the focus of the conference. However, scores for explaining offender rights and checking for understanding were lower for cases conducted after May 1, 1996. Overall, the proportion of conferences missing one of the preamble components increased from 22 percent to 34 percent following the in-service training.

However, the proportion of conferences where the facilitator either influenced the outcomes or lectured the offenders dropped from 70 percent to 48 percent following the in-service training. The authoritarian tone of the conferences was dramatically reduced by providing the corrective feedback. Because the total number of mistakes grew, it suggests that as officers became more comfortable with conferencing, they tended to improvise on the conference script and miss important pieces of the preamble.

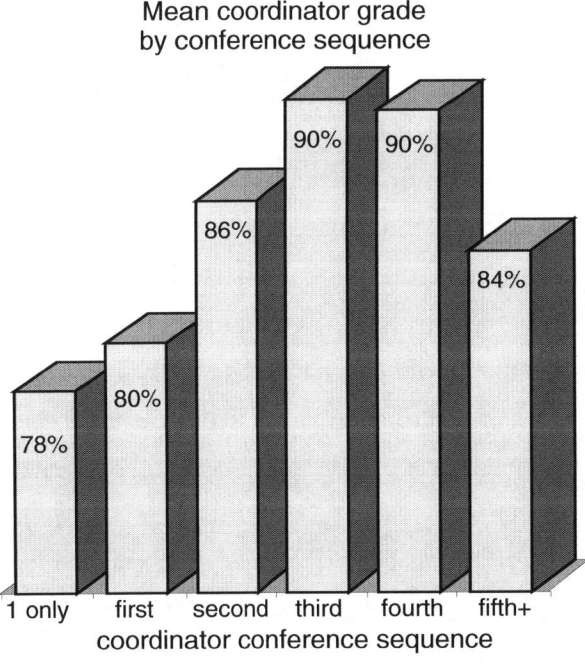

Exhibit 17
Mean coordinator grade by conference sequence

To test improvement in individual officers' performance over time, it is necessary to compare first conference performance with subsequent conferences. There were 19 officers who conducted the 56 conferences observed. Five officers conducted 1 conference, four officers conducted 2, three conducted 3, two conducted 4, four conducted 5 and one conducted 6 conferences. Officer performance was scored with an overall grade and the number of conference participants as described above.

As shown in Exhibit 17, the average grade for officers conducting only one conference ($n = 5$) was no lower than the first conference conducted by other officers ($n = 14$). The average grade increased for the second conference conducted ($n = 14$) and again for the third conference ($n = 10$). However, the grade peaked at 93 percent for the fourth conference ($n = 7$) and appears to have declined for the fifth and sixth conference ($n = 6$). Given the small number of cases involved, these differences are not statistically significant.

Since officers were encouraged to conduct larger conferences at the in-service, this prompting appears to have had an effect, as shown in Exhibit 18. There was an average of 5.4 participants for facilitators' first conferences (whether or not they conducted additional conferences). Following the in-service training, the average number of participants increased to 6.6 for officer's second conferences. However, the size of the conferences continued to decline with subsequent conferences.

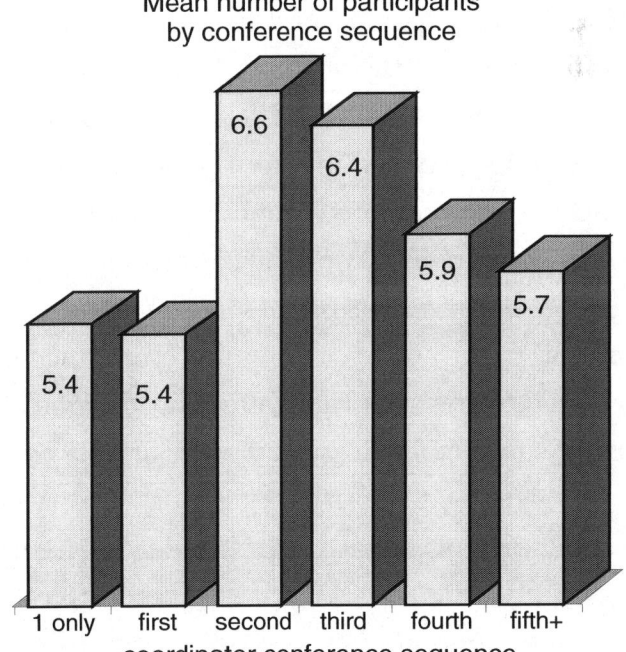

Exhibit 18
Mean number of participants by conference sequence

Because of the small number of cases available for a within-facilitator analysis, none of these differences are statistically significant. These results are suggestive rather than definitive. There appears to have been an improvement in officers' performance after the in-service training and after the five officers dropped out of the program. Overall grades appear to improve with experience up to the third conference. In-service training did improve performance, and such meetings might best be planned before the fourth or fifth conference. These results are consistent with a need for ongoing evaluation and regular in-service feedback.

An analysis was conducted examining relationships between the measures from the conference observations and other variables available in the study. First, variables related to conference composition (time to conference, length of conference, number of participants, and the presence of the arresting officer) were examined. The longer the period from crime to conference, the more likely the victim judged the process as fair, $r(46) = .33$, $p < .05$. The longer the conference took, the more likely the offender felt that their opinion had been adequately considered, $r(45) = .35$, $p < .05$. Retail theft cases took less time to run, $r(55) = -.64$, $p < .001$, had fewer participants, $r(56) = -.46$, $p < .001$, and were less likely to include the arresting officer, $r(56) = -.37$, $p < .01$. Among these variables, only days to conference was related to the in-service training, $r(56) = .28$, $p < .05$, with the time from crime to conference being greater after the in-service. The conference composition variables (total participants, presence of other young people, and presence of arresting officer) were unrelated to other participant perception variables or outcome variables.

The offender was less likely to report being held accountable when facilitators failed to introduce participants, failed to set the focus, made suggestions about the outcome or affected the outcome, $r(47) = .38$, $r(47) = .38$, $r(47) = .40$ and $r(47) = .46$, respectively, all $p < .01$. When the facilitators were inappropriate, $r(56) = -.40$, $p < .01$, failed to maintain the distinction between person and behavior, $r(56) = -.57$, $p < .001$, affected the conference outcome, $r(56) = -.28$, $p < .05$, or failed to adhere to protocol, $r(56) = -.37$, $p < .05$, the observers reported less offender remorse. Adherence to conference protocol was positively related to the family assuming responsibility for the offenders' behavior, $r(56) = .28$, $p < .05$. None of these protocol variables were related to offender, victim or parent satisfaction with how the case was handled, or to agreement compliance or recidivism.

Observer ratings of victim satisfaction was positively related to the number of participants, $r(56) = .27$, $p < .05$, and compliance with protocol, $r(56) = .38$, $p < .01$), and negatively related to the facilitator affecting the outcome, $r(56) = -.42$, $p < .01$. Observer ratings of victims' sense of forgiveness was positively related to the facilitator protocol score, $r(56) = .34$, $p < .05$, and facilitators maintaining the distinction between person and behavior, $r(56) = .30$, $p < .05$; and was negatively related to officer suggesting or affecting the outcome, $r(56) = -.30$, $p < .05$ and $r(56) = -.38$, $p < .01$, respectively. There was a positive relationship between observer ratings of victim satisfaction and sense of forgiveness at the end of the conference and the victims' self-reported satisfaction later, $r(46) = .32, p < .05$ and $r(46) = .31, p < .05$, respectively. Finally, observer ratings of victim satisfaction or sense of forgiveness was unrelated to offender compliance with agreement or recidivism.

The higher the observers rated the offender sense of remorse, the more likely the victim rated the offender as being held adequately accountable, $r(56) = .32, p < .05$. The higher the observers rated the offender understanding of the harm caused, the more likely the victim rated the system as fair, $r(46) = .31, p < .05$. There was a positive relationship between how satisfied the offender said he was with the way his case was handled and his showing of remorse, $r(48) = .36, p < .05$, ending with a sense of pride, $r(48) = .37, p < .01$, and the amount of reintegration after the conference, $r(48) = .36, p < .05$. Victims were more likely to report that their opinion was considered when the offender seemed to understand the harm, $r(46) = .42, p < .01$, expressed remorse, $r(46) = .45, p < .01$, and ended the conference with a sense of pride, $r(46) = .30, p < .05$. The more punitive the conference was rated, the less the victim felt their own opinion was considered, $r(46) = -.39, p < .01$. Among these observer-rated variables, offender expression of remorse was positively related to compliance with the agreement, $r(56) = .30, p < .05$. Also, the more the offender's family volunteered future responsibility for the offender's behavior, the more likely the offender is to comply with the agreement, $r(56) = .29, p < .05$, and the less likely the offender is to have a future arrest, $r(56) = -.28, p < .05$.

Finally, whether or not the offender complied with the agreement was related to how accountable they felt they had been held, $r(47) = .38, p < .01$, how fair the offender, $r(40) = .37, p < .01$, and victim, $r(44) = .37, p < .01$, felt the process was, how satisfied the offender was, $r(48) = .53, p < .01$, how fair the offender thought the conference was to the victim, $r(39) = .37, p < .05$, and whether the offender felt their own opinion had adequately been considered, $r(46) = .38, p < .05$. Whether the offender was rearrested after the conference was related to their experience of fairness, $r(47) = .34, p < .05$, whether offenders felt their opinion had been considered, $r(46) = .34, p < .05$, and whether offenders felt it had been their own choice to participate in the conference, $r(47) = .34, p < .05$. None of the compliance or recidivism outcomes differed across crime type, age or gender of offender, or period of the experiment.

The observers were also asked to judge which participant was most punitive at each conference. As shown in Exhibit 19, the parents of the offenders were seen as the most punitive in 33 percent of the conferences, the victim or victim supporter in 22 percent, and others in 10 percent of the conferences. In 35 percent of observed conferences, no participant could be identified as punitive at all.

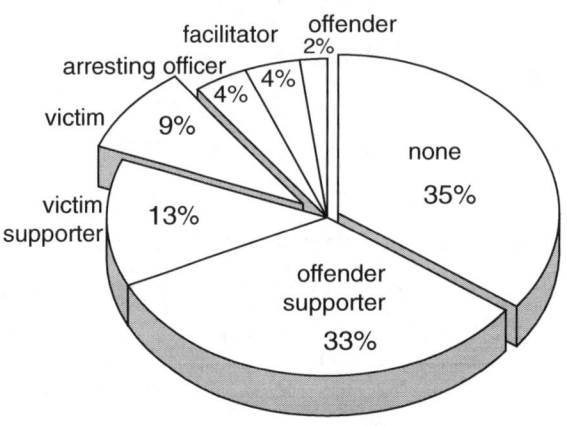

Exhibit 19
Observer ratings of most punitive participant

- facilitator 2%
- offender 2%
- arresting officer 4%
- victim 9%
- victim supporter 13%
- none 35%
- offender supporter 33%

Conference Outcomes

There were 80 offenders involved in 64 conferences. Of the offenders, 70 percent committed property crimes and 30 percent violent crimes. There were 48 conferenced offenders charged with retail theft, 10 with disorderly conduct, 13 with harassment, 6 with criminal mischief, 2 with theft, and 1 with noise-a-nuisance. One of the 80 offenders, besides going through a conference, also made a guilty plea at the district court without the knowledge of the police department.

Fifty-three percent of conferenced offenders were male, 47 percent female. They were primarily Hispanic (51 percent) and white (41 percent). Of the remaining 8 percent, 1 was black and 5 were other races. Eighty-nine percent were residents of the city of Bethlehem—33 percent from Zip1, 36 percent from Zip2, and 20 percent from Zip3—with the other 11 percent from surrounding suburbs.

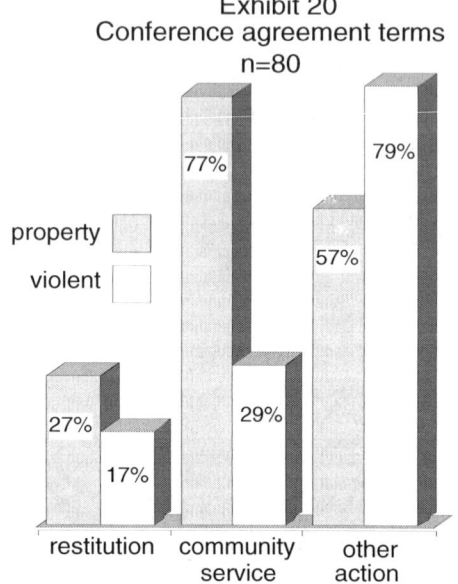

As shown in Exhibit 20, the types of outcomes from conferences varied by type of offense. Of the agreements reached in conferences for property crimes, 27 percent included payment of restitution, 77 percent included community service, and 57 percent included some other reparative action. For violent crimes cases, 17 percent included payment, 29 percent included community service, and 79 percent included some other reparative action. Property cases were nearly three times more likely to include community service as a condition of the agreement than violent cases, $\chi^2 (1, n=80) = 16.3, p < .0001$. The average amount of community service was 24 hours, ranging from 2 to 100 hours ($SD = 19.4, n = 50$). For property cases, the average amount was 26 hours ($SD = 20.0, n = 43$). For violent cases, it was 11 hours ($SD = 3.5, n = 7$). The amount of community service for property cases was nearly three times higher than for violent cases among those offenders agreeing to community service as part of the conference contract, $F(1, 48) = 4.2, p < .05$.

The average amount of restitution payments was $124.95, ranging from $28 to $233 ($SD = 56.3, n = 19$). For property cases, the average payment was $136.87 ($SD = 33.5, n = 15$). As shown in Exhibit 21, restitution was higher for property cases than it was for violent cases. For violent cases, it was $80.25 ($SD = 101.8, n = 4$). This was not a significant difference. Payments were either restitution for damages or losses incurred ($n = 8$), or $150 civil demand payments for retail theft ($n = 11$).

The most common action other than community service and restitution was the offender agreeing to write personal letters of apology ($n = 24$) and making personal apologies ($n = 8$). The other types of reparative actions were meeting together to discuss the problem

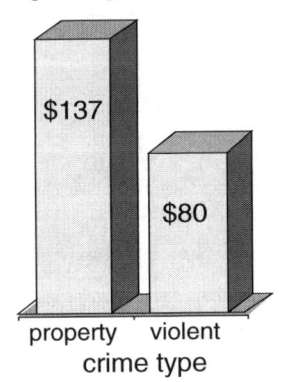

Exhibit 21
Average restitution for cases agreeing to restitution

further ($n = 4$), being referred to counseling or youth services ($n = 4$), avoiding contact with a person ($n = 4$), attending counseling ($n = 3$), promising not to re-offend ($n = 3$), attending English tutoring ($n = 2$), aiding a teacher in class ($n = 1$), taking a tour of prison ($n = 1$), having a structured summer ($n = 1$), and adhering to a behavior contract ($n = 1$).

There was an attempt by the participants, especially in the violent cases, to fashion specific reparative action which attempted to address a source of difficulty for offenders. Some retailers were constrained by their company policy to seek compliance with the civil claim and did not have the authority to alter that condition. These retailer representatives were sometimes satisfied with the offender agreement to "not contest" that civil action, and sometimes they asked for letters of apology in addition. Two of the large retail stores regularly asked for 40 hours of community service and included new security personnel in their conferences as victim supporters as part of their in-service training.

In spite of the varied conditions of the agreements in conferences involving a various amount of offender time and energy, all but five of the 80 offenders (94 percent) complied with their agreements, which replicates Moore's original Wagga findings. Four of the five compliance failures were retail theft; the other was the first case conferenced in the project. Three retail theft offenders failed to show for their community service and had their cases referred to court, and the other retail theft case pled guilty after the conference so he was not held to his agreement contract. The offender charged with harassment who failed to comply with washing ten police cars was rearrested over conflict involving the same victim after agreeing to avoid her and had his case referred to court for disposition. Therefore, the conference compliance rates were 93 percent for property cases and 96 percent for violent cases.

Conclusions

The initial training received by the police conducting conferences was insufficient to make it clear to officers the purpose of restorative conferences. While they easily picked up the mechanics of the scripted process, an in-service training was necessary early in the experiment to reinforce the reintegrative intention of the conferences. Officers were less likely to lecture or interfere with agreement conditions following this retraining session. However, some felt uncomfortable reading directly from the script and therefore had a tendency to miss some important parts of the process. Overall, the facilitators complied with conference protocol in nearly 90 percent of the conferences following the in-service. Facilitator performance improved with each officer's subsequent conferences.

Conferences were held an average of 34 days after the offense, had an average of 6 participants and took an average of 34 minutes with 5 minutes social time. Retail theft conferences were 20 minutes shorter than other conferences. Conferences for property crimes had an average of three fewer participants, were more likely to involve payment of restitution, and were more likely to include community service. The community service for conferenced property cases was also greater than conferences for violent cases.

There were a number of important differences between the specific type of criminal offense conferenced. Since 60 percent of conferences were for retail theft, most crime victims participating in the conferences were retail stores. Individuals were the victims in only 23 percent of all the conferences. Schools were the victims of record for 54 percent of the violent crimes, many involving a fight between students who were mutually charged with fighting on school grounds.

Conferences involving a personal victim or fights at school had a very different character than retail theft conferences. These conferences had a greater expression of emotion and a higher sense of reintegration between participants. Agreements fashioned for violent offenders included fewer and lesser sanctions, were more likely to involve only an apology, and were more individualized, with personal service rather than community service.

Conferencing appears to work better with violent offenses, yet conferencing for property offenses is still beneficial, especially where a personal victim can be identified. Conferences between mutual antagonists appear to produce the most restorative process, regardless of the age, gender, race or language of the participants involved.

4
Police Surveys

The study of police-based conferencing in Wagga Wagga, New South Wales, Australia, suggested that the program had significant effects on changing the attitude and orientation of the police department, from a punitive, legalistic approach to a problem-solving, restorative approach (Moore, 1995). The present study empirically tested this assertion by examining how police attitudes and role orientation changed as a result of a number of officers conducting restorative conferences. An officer attitudinal and work environmental survey was administered to the Bethlehem Police Department on two occasions, just before the conferencing program commenced (pre-test) and eighteen months later (post-test).

Methods

Participants

At the time of the pre-test, the Bethlehem Police Department had a total of 132 police, including 98 line-level officers (60 percent), 17 sergeants (13 percent), 5 detectives (4 percent), 7 lieutenants (5 percent), 3 captains (2 percent), and one commissioner (1 percent) and deputy commissioner (1 percent). Most of the 98 line-level officers were in patrol divisions (68 percent); the others were divided among community service (11 percent), traffic (5 percent), staff-administration (2 percent), investigations (6 percent) and special operations (7 percent). There were three female officers. Officers' ages ranged from 23 years to 63 years ($M = 39.3$, $SD = 9.5$), and their length of service in Bethlehem ranged from 1 to 36 years ($M = 13.4$, $SD = 9.7$). At pre-test time, 60 percent of the department had only a high school diploma, 16 percent had an associate degree, and 24 percent had a bachelor degree.

At the time of the post-test, the composition of the Bethlehem Police Department was largely the same. There was a 5 percent increase in personnel to a total of 140 officers as the result of retirements and new hires. The proportion of the personnel were distributed much the same as at pre-test time. There was only one female officer at the time of the post-test. The one female officer trained in conferencing was no longer with the department. The department was slightly older ($M = 40.7$, $SD = 9.4$) and more experienced ($M = 13.5$, $SD = 10.0$). At post-test time, the department was also slightly better educated, with 29 percent of the department having a bachelor degree, 16 percent an associate degree, and 56 percent a high school diploma.

Eighteen Bethlehem police officers—17 line-level officers and one lieutenant—were trained to conduct family group conferences as part of the experiment. Two additional line-level officers had been trained previously. This group of 20 trained officers differed significantly from the rest of the department in that officers trained were on average 6.5 years younger, $t(130) = 2.9$, $p < .01$, and had on average 6.8 fewer years of experience $t(130) = 3.0$, $p < .01$, than those who were not trained.

Apparatus

The survey developed for this project was a combination of two sets of scales reported reliable in previously published studies. The first set of scales was the 112-item Police Daily Hassles scales and the 82-item Police Uplifts scales as reported by Hart, Wearing and Headey (1993, 1994). They created these scales to measure the positive and negative work-related experiences common to police officers, as part of an exploration into understanding how a person's well-being is determined by multivariate relationships within a work environment. These scales were developed from a systematic sample of 330 officers drawn from all ranks and work sections within the Victoria Police Department in Australia. The construct validity of the scales was supported by a series of factor analyses and cross-validated on a second sample of 404 police officers. Each of these scales was divided into operational and organizational items, hassles and uplifts scales and specific item subscales.

Overall Hassles and Uplifts scales were found to be somewhat more reliable among the Bethlehem Police than reported in either study by Hart, Wearing & Headey. This was true for Operational and Organizational Hassles and Uplifts scales. As shown in Exhibit 22, all six of the overall scales and 23 of the 31 subscales were found to be reliable on both the pre- and post-tests samples (*alpha* > .60). Six subscales failed to maintain reliability on the pre-test and five on the post-test. Hassles from equipment and complaints, and uplifts from rosters were unreliable only on the pre-test; hassles from supervision and uplifts from equipment were unreliable only on the post-test; and hassles from promotions and uplifts from

Exhibit 22a
Reliability of Hassles and Uplifts Scales

HASSLES SCALES RELIABILITY	Bethlehem Pre-test $n=75$		Bethlehem Post-test $n=51$		Hart, et al. '90 $n=1,130$	Hart, et al. '88 $n=330$	
	Alpha	Means	Alpha	Means	Alpha	Alpha	Means
Hassles	0.97	2.4	0.97	2.3	0.87	0.91	1.7
Organizational Hassles	0.96	2.5	0.96	2.5	0.81	0.87	1.7
Communication	0.82	2.4	0.83	2.5	0.83	0.88	1.5
Morale	0.71	2.2	0.70	2.1	0.83	0.83	1.4
Co-workers	0.88	2.8	0.90	2.9	0.93	0.93	1.7
Ratings	0.91	2.7	0.98	2.5	0.86	0.79	1.8
Supervision	0.64	2.1	0.57	2.0	0.72	0.80	1.3
Administration	0.87	2.9	0.90	2.9	0.90	0.93	2.0
Individual	0.79	2.3	0.81	2.2	0.86	0.88	1.7
Amenities	0.63	2.1	0.63	2.1	0.89	0.87	1.9
Equipment	0.56	2.4	0.66	2.6	0.81	0.86	2.2
Promotions	0.52	1.8	0.49	1.7	0.89	0.93	1.7
Operational Hassles	0.94	2.3	0.95	2.3	0.78	0.83	1.6
Danger	0.85	1.9	0.81	1.8	0.90	0.81	1.0
Victims	0.84	2.2	0.79	2.1	0.90	0.89	1.3
Frustration	0.79	2.6	0.80	2.4	0.85	0.86	1.6
External	0.77	2.6	0.84	2.5	0.86	0.90	1.8
Activity	0.83	2.3	0.88	2.2	0.88	0.88	1.6
Complaints	0.55	2.6	0.70	2.6	0.82	0.80	1.7
People	0.62	2.4	0.75	2.4	0.85	0.77	1.8
Workload	0.86	2.4	0.88	2.4	0.88	0.82	1.7
Driving	0.70	2.5	0.84	2.4	0.77	0.82	2.2

Exhibit 22b
Reliability of Hassles and Uplifts Scales

UPLIFTS SCALES RELIABILITY	Bethlehem Pre-test n = 75		Bethlehem Post-test n = 51		Hart, et al. '90 n = 1,130	Hart, et al. '88 n = 330	
	Alpha	Means	Alpha	Means	Alpha	Alpha	Means
Uplifts	0.96	3.3	0.96	3.2	0.80	0.77	2.7
Organizational Uplifts	0.95	3.4	0.94	3.3	0.83	0.81	2.8
Amenities	0.72	2.9	0.79	2.9	0.90	0.79	2.8
Co-workers	0.90	3.7	0.88	3.6	0.91	0.92	3.1
Administration	0.45	3.1	0.29	3.0	0.86	0.85	2.1
Decision-making	0.75	3.6	0.85	3.5	0.82	0.88	3.0
Supervision	0.81	3.5	0.79	3.3	0.83	0.77	2.8
Workload	0.82	3.7	0.72	3.4	0.81	0.79	3.0
Equipment	0.92	3.4	0.34	3.6	0.93	0.92	2.6
Family	0.49	3.1	0.35	3.3	0.67	0.52	2.8
Promotions	0.72	3.0	0.71	3.1	0.88	0.87	2.6
Operational Uplifts	0.88	3.2	0.93	3.0	0.73	0.65	2.3
Offenders	0.84	3.0	0.89	2.7	0.94	0.92	1.9
Victims	0.85	3.5	0.92	3.1	0.94	0.90	2.3
Rosters	0.49	3.3	0.72	3.2	0.83	0.67	2.8

administration and family were unreliable on both pre- and post-tests.

The second set of scales used to measure changes in the Bethlehem Police was taken from a study examining factors influencing the attitudes of police officers toward their roles and communities. These scales were developed with 761 officers employed by two large police departments in the Washington, D.C. metropolitan area (Brooks, Piquero & Cronin, 1993). While this study did not report reliability coefficients, the present study found that five of the nine scales produced adequate reliability ratings in both pre-test and post-test (*alpha* > .60). A scale measuring perception of community support was deemed reliable in the pre-test but unreliable in the post-test. A scale measuring belief in police discretion was unreliable in the pre-test but reliable in the post-test. Scales measuring perception of the quality of police services and orientation toward force had inadequate reliability ratings in both pre- and post-tests (see Exhibit 23).

Two scales measuring police orientation toward their roles and two scales measuring

Exhibit 23
Police attitude scales reliability

ATTITUDES SCALES RELIABILITY	Bethlehem Pre-Test n = 75		Bethlehem Post-Test n = 51		Brooks, et al. n = 330
	Alpha	Means	Alpha	Means	Means
Crime Control Orientation	0.71	2.9	0.72	2.8	2.9
Service Orientation	0.69	3.5	0.80	3.5	3.2
Perception of Community Support	0.63	2.8	0.41	3.2	2.7
Perception of Community Cooperation	0.69	64%	0.87	61%	64%
Belief in Police Discretion	0.55	3.5	0.85	3.3	3.6
Perception of CJ System Support	0.67	3.6	0.61	3.4	3.0
Perception of the Quality of Police Services	0.57	3.8	0.55	3.8	3.5
Orientation Toward Force	0.41	2.9	0.33	2.7	3.1
Orientation Toward Police Solidarity	0.86	3.0	0.81	3.0	3.3

police attitudes toward their work activities were developed using factor analysis of the combined pre-test elements of both survey items (see Exhibit 24). The two scales measuring orientation toward police roles were (1) the Authority Scale, measuring the degree to which officers felt that police generally require more formal authority, and (2) the Service Scale, measuring the degree to which officers felt that police generally should provide service assistance to citizens. The two scales measuring attitudes toward their specific tasks were (1) the Arrest Scale, measuring positive attitudes toward activities involved in exercising formal authority, and (2) the Helping Scale, measuring positive attitudes toward helping citizens through actual provision of service activities. All of these scales held their reliability on the post-test sample, except the Authority Scale.

The items in the Authority Scale were:
1) Police should handle public nuisance problems (4-point item)
2) Police should help settle family disputes (4-point item)
3) Policing should be seen as a service organization (4-point item)

Exhibit 24
Police orientation scales reliability

CONSTRUCTED POLICE ORIENTATION SCALES	Pre-Test n = 75		Post-Test n = 51	
	alpha	mean	alpha	mean
Authority	0.75	2.64	0.48	2.63
Service	0.71	3.49	0.71	3.51
Arrest	0.84	2.98	0.89	2.72
Helping	0.89	3.54	0.92	3.12

The items in the Service Scale were:
1) Many of the decisions by the Supreme Court interfere with the ability of police to fight crime (4-point item)
2) Officers would be more effective if they didn't have to worry about "probable cause" requirements for searching citizens (4-point item)
3) If police officers in high crime areas had fewer restrictions on their use of force, many of the serious crime problems in those neighborhoods would be greatly reduced (4-point item)
4) Lack of police powers (5-point hassle item)

The items in the Arrest Scale were:
1) Getting a good result at court (5-point uplift item)
2) Getting a good "pinch" (5-point uplift item)
3) Going to good calls (5-point uplift item)
4) Charging someone (5-point uplift item)
5) Obtaining an admission from a crook (5-point uplift item)
6) Going on a raid (5-point uplift item)

The items in the Helping Scale were:
1) Helping the public (5-point uplift item)
2) Helping children (5-point uplift item)
3) Helping complainants (5-point uplift item)
4) Helping motorists (5-point uplift item)

Five-point ordinal items measuring knowledge and support of family group conferencing for moderately serious juvenile offenses were also included in the questionnaire. In addition, on the post-test questionnaire, there were five-point ordinal items measuring support of family group conferencing for use with domestic dispute calls and for moderately serious adult offenses.

Two additional scales measuring exposure to conferencing and support for conferencing were developed (see Exhibit 25), which were both found to be reliable on the post-test sample (*alpha* > .60).

The Exposure Scale had two items:
1) How much an officer knew about conferencing (5-point item)
2) Whether an officer had conducted a conference (dichotomous item)

The Support scale had three items:
1) Level of support for conferencing for moderately serious juvenile offenders (5-point item)
2) Level of support for conferencing for moderately serious adult offenders (5-point item)
3) Level of support for conferencing for responding to domestic dispute calls (5-point item)

Exhibit 25
Conferencing scales reliability

CONFERENCING SCALES	n = 51	
	alpha	mean
Exposure	0.75	2.63
Support	0.84	9.43

Procedure

Surveys were distributed to all members of the Bethlehem Police Department during roll calls. Officers were required to give identifying information in the form of badge number but were informed, in a cover letter signed by the commissioner and the research director, that their survey responses would be kept confidential and would not be shown to police administration. Stamped return envelopes addressed to the research director were included with all surveys. The surveys were non-anonymous to allow matching of pre-test and post-test scores for each respondent. This matched-subjects design allows for a more powerful test of difference than a between-groups design.

Seventy-seven of the 131 (59 percent) officers on the force responded to the pre-test. The response rate on the post-test declined with only 51 of the 139 total (36 percent) responding. The overall response rates for the pre- and post-tests were deemed adequate, with a response rate for the pre-test exceeding those reported in two of the other studies using anonymous versions of these questionnaires (Hart, Wearing & Headey, 1993; Brooks, Piquero & Cronin, 1993), and the post-test response equaling that of one of these other studies (Hart, Wearing & Headey, 1994), as shown in Exhibit 26.

Analysis of response bias across years of experience, age, rank and education demonstrated that those who responded were generally representative of the force as a whole. The only significant difference between respondents and non-respondents was in the pre-test. Officers with 5 or fewer years of service and a college degree were more likely to respond than other officers, $\chi^2 (1, n = 37) = 5.8, p < .05$. Feedback from those refusing to complete the survey suggested that they primarily objected to questions relating to police solidarity (e.g., "would you arrest fellow officers who . . . ?").

To assess retest response bias, those who responded to both surveys and those who responded to the pre-test only were compared by years of experience, age, rank and education. The only significant difference between pre-test sample and post-test sample was that

Exhibit 26
Police survey response rates

Survey	#police	responses	response rate
Bethlehem Police Pre-Test	131	77	59%
Bethlehem Police Post-Test	139	51	36%
Hart, et al. #1	491	340	67%
Hart, et al. #2	1130	404	36%
Brooks, et al.	1384	761	55%

there was a higher proportion of line-level officers and a lower proportion of sergeants and detectives and lieutenants and above who responded to both surveys versus the pre-test only, $\chi^2 (2, n = 71) = 6.5, p < .05$. There were no other significant differences in years of experience, age, rank and education based on whether someone responded to both pre- and post-tests, pre-test only, post-test only or neither.

Thus, the response bias for the two surveys was deemed minimal. The newer officers were somewhat over-represented in the pre-test and line-level officers were somewhat over-represented in the matched pre-post sample. Officers trained in conferencing were equally likely to respond to the survey as other officers in the department.

As a further test of the possibility of a response bias, a series of t-tests were conducted comparing the pre-test scores for the pre-test only group and the pre-post matched group on the 50 Hassles and Uplifts and Police Attitudes scales. The only scale showing a significant difference in means between groups was the attitude scale measuring perception of community support, $t(73.7) = -2.2, p < .05$. This suggests that those who responded to the pre-test but not the post-test had a slightly more favorable perception of community support than those who responded to both the pre-test and post-test. However, given the number of t-tests conducted, finding one of 50 tests significant could be accounted for by chance alone. Therefore, there was essentially no bias in pre-test scores between those who responded to the pre-test only and those who responded to both pre- and post-tests.

Results

Of the 75 pre-test respondents, 44 percent said they knew nothing about family group conferencing, 20 percent heard about it, 28 percent knew a little, 5 percent knew quite a bit, and 3 percent knew a great deal. Of the 51 post-test respondents, 14 percent said they knew nothing about family group conferencing, 18 percent heard about it, 39 percent knew a little, 22 percent knew quite a bit, and 8 percent knew a great deal (see Exhibit 27).

There was a significant increase in how much officers said they knew about conferencing, $t(34) = 4.9, p < .001$. However, there was no overall significant change in support for family group conferencing for moderately serious juvenile offenses. While knowledge of conferencing increased over the course of the experiment, support for conferencing did not on a department-wide basis.

Paired t-tests of pre- and post-test scores were conducted on all 50 scales to determine if there was any change in police attitudes and perceptions of the role of police during the experimental period. Only perception of community support changed significantly, indicating a moderate increase in how police perceived the community's support of their department, $t(34) = -2.2$, $p < .05$. Given the number of t-tests conducted and the lack of reliability of this measure on the post-test, this too may have been due to chance alone. Thus, conferencing cannot be said to have had a significant impact on changing police attitudes toward their activities or the role of police.

In spite of the lack of a systemic effect, it is possible that there were changes at the individual level for some officers, based on their exposure to and support for conferencing. Using partial correlations, an analysis was conducted to determine if there were significant changes in scores for the Police Attitudes and Hassles and Uplifts scales based on scores for the Exposure scale and the Support scale.

Exhibit 27
Knowledge of conferencing

The Exposure scale was significantly correlated with Perception of Community Cooperation and Orientation Toward the Use of Force, $r(32) = .44$, $p < .05$ and $r(32) = -.37$, $p < .05$, respectively. Because of the relationship between conducting conferences and age and years of experience, the partial correlations were run again controlling for these variables. The correlations remained significant. Because Orientation Toward Force was unreliable on both pre-test and post-test, caution must be used in interpreting relationships involving these scales. As shown in Exhibit 28, those with a higher exposure to conferencing had a moderate increase in Perception of Community Cooperation and as shown in Exhibit 29, those with a higher exposure to conferencing had a decrease in Orientation Toward the Use of Force.

The Support scale was significantly correlated with Crime Control Orientation and Individual Hassles. However, controlling for age and years of experience, only the correlation with Crime Control Orientation remained significant, $r(30) = -.54$, $p < .01$ as shown in Exhibit 30.

Paired t-tests were run on pre- and post-test scores among those who conducted family group conferences. There was a significant increase in Perception of Community Cooperation, $t(8) = -2.5$, $p < .05$, a moderate decrease in Uplift From Administration, $t(8) = 3.6$, $p < .01$, and a moderate decrease in Uplift From Workload, $t(8) = 4.3$, $p < .01$.

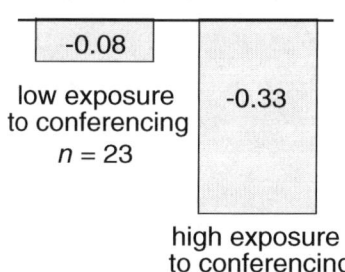

Exhibit 28
Mean change in orientation toward the use of force

Nonparametric tests were conducted using pre- and posttest scores of those who had conducted conferences ($n = 9$) for several individual items (4 Hassle/Uplift and 4 Attitudes items) which were deemed likely to change because of exposure to conducting restorative conferences: helping children (uplift), handling juveniles (hassle), dealing with parents (hassle), thanks from the public (uplift), police should help settle family disputes, people in Bethlehem lack respect for police, police should not handle social or personal problems, young people in Bethlehem respect police. There were no significant changes in these items.

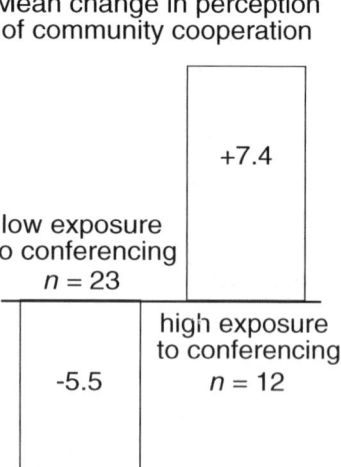

Exhibit 29
Mean change in perception of community cooperation

low exposure to conferencing $n = 23$: +7.4

high exposure to conferencing $n = 12$: -5.5

Exhibit 30
Mean change in crime control orientation

low support for conferencing $n = 19$: +0.14

high support for conferencing $n = 16$: -0.34

Conclusions

It appears that although there were no significant changes in attitudes and role perceptions over the entire Bethlehem Police Department during the course of the experiment, there were some significant changes observed among those with the most exposure to conferencing. Those who knew more about conferencing and had conducted conferences showed significant increases in their perceptions of community cooperation and a significant decrease in their orientation toward a crime control approach to policing. This suggests movement toward an approach to policing more consistent with problem-oriented policing and community policing among those who were exposed to and supportive of conferencing. Based on these analyses, it is likely that as more officers are exposed to conferencing, these effects will become more widespread in the Bethlehem Police Department.

It is perhaps not surprising that there were no systematic changes in the perceptions of officers who were not directly involved in conferencing. There appear to be officers who are oriented toward use of force and crime control activities who do not feel that conferencing is "real" police work. However, the "police culture" is not a single perspective, with more and more officers recognizing the importance of problem-solving and providing community services as essential parts of real police work. Rather than change everyone's minds, experience with conferencing appears to draw its supporters and find its detractors among the same groups who support or oppose community policing in general.

5
Participant Surveys

An important part of this study was to assess how victims, offenders and the community would react to a restorative policing strategy such as conferencing and also to get a sense of people's affinity to restorative justice principles. Part of this assessment would involve exploring how perceptions of conferencing compared to perceptions of formal adjudication procedures. Surveys were developed for victims, offenders and parents of offenders who had either gone through a conference or through formal adjudication processes to collect data on people's perceptions of how their cases were handled and their general views of the nature of justice. Those who participated in conferences received a different questionnaire than those whose cases went through formal adjudication, with some similar questions to allow for comparison and some questions particular to the type of case processing.

Methods

Participants

There were 215 criminal incidents included in the study. These involved the arrest of 292 juveniles and the victimization of 217 victims: 85 individuals, 107 retail stores, and 25 schools. Some retail stores and schools were the victims in multiple cases, but were treated separately for each criminal incident.

Offenders. Offenders assigned to the control group, offenders who declined to participate, and offenders whose victim declined to participate were processed through the normal adjudicatory process. Offenders charged with summary offenses are required to appear and enter a plea before the district magistrate in the jurisdiction where the offense took place. Offenders charged with a misdemeanor or felony have their cases referred for intake to the juvenile court probation department of the county where the offense took place. Some offenders have their charge dropped by the police (non-arrest) or by the magistrate (withdrawn or dismissed), especially when requested by the complainant. As shown in Exhibit 31, 52 percent of the 292 offenders in this study had their cases handled by a district magistrate (dropped, guilty plea, guilty trial, or not guilty), 9 percent were disposed by juvenile probation (supervision or informal adjustment), and 8 percent had not yet been disposed. The other 32 percent were disposed by the police (counsel & release or conference).

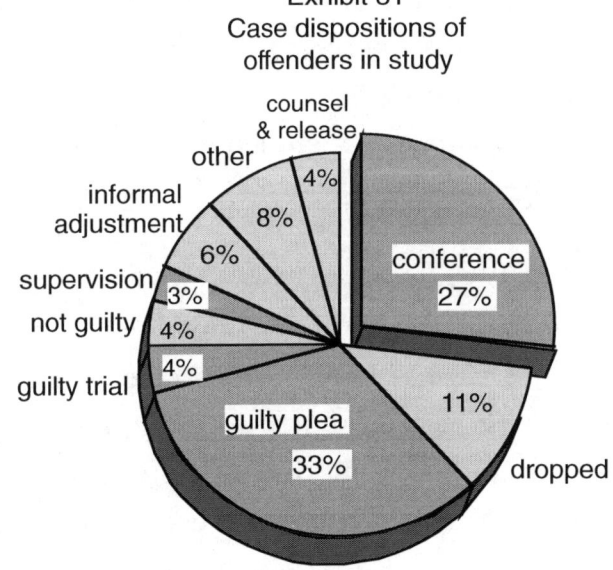

Exhibit 31
Case dispositions of offenders in study

Parents. Parents of juvenile offenders are often as much victimized by their child's behavior as is the actual victim. Parents of offenders are required to pick up their child from the police station after arrest processing is completed. The call from the police that their child has been arrested is just the beginning of a series of emotional hurdles they must face. Parents whose children must appear before the magistrate usually accompany their child and are often given an opportunity to speak. Parents of offenders whose cases are conferenced had to agree to let their child participate in the program and to accompany their child at the conference. Parents were generally very responsive to the idea of a restorative conference and seemed to have a better understanding than their child of the advantage of avoiding a juvenile record. In many ways, parents of young offenders are in a much better position to evaluate the justness of the process than are their misbehaving children.

Victims. Victims of juvenile crime are generally also the complainants to the police. To a certain extent, then, victims are the "customers" of police services. The crime victims in this study differed in a number of respects from the broader population of crime victims. First, the victims included in this study could identify their offenders. Second, these offenders had been arrested by the police. Third, the offenders were all juveniles. Because of these factors, we cannot confidently generalize findings to the entire population of crime victims, nor to the population of victims of juvenile crime. However, we can regard this sample as representative of the population of victims of lesser juvenile crime with a known offender who has been arrested. There is no reason to suspect that this subpopulation of victims in Bethlehem, Pennsylvania, differs in important ways from such victims in other mid-sized American cities. In interpreting the results, however, we must take the limitations of the sample population into account.

There is an additional consideration in interpreting the results of this survey. Among the victims responding to the survey, victims of violent crimes were much more likely to have known the offender before the conference (77 percent) compared to victims of property crimes (5 percent). Differences between crime types and between personal versus institutional victims are relevant for both the generalizability of these results to other crime victims not included in this study as well as generalizing to similar victims in other localities.

Apparatus

Surveys were developed using questionnaires from Mark Umbreit's book, *Victim Meets Offender* (1994). Questions related to perceptions of how the case was handled by the justice system, attitudes and beliefs about the justice system, attitudes toward the victim and offender, attitudes toward how the particular case was handled and perceptions of fairness. Surveys were available in English and Spanish translations because of the large Spanish-speaking population in Bethlehem. Originally, surveys had only been developed for victims and offenders, but it became apparent that offenders' parents were often enthusiastic about conferencing and sometimes completing their child's survey themselves. Thus, a separate offender's parent survey was developed (see research instruments in appendix).

Procedure

Each victim, offender and offender's parent was sent a questionnaire following the disposition of their case, whether it was diverted through a restorative justice conference, disposed in magistrate court for summary offenses, or disposed in juvenile court for misdemeanors.

The original intent was to send surveys to subjects approximately two weeks after the disposition of the case. This did not occur in practice. The actual time from disposition to sending the survey varied. It was longer for court-adjudicated cases because information on times of disposition was not usually available from the magistrate immediately after disposition and required searching a computer database. Conferenced cases were tracked by the Bethlehem Police for agreement compliance; therefore, current address information was readily available for these cases. In no cases were participants sent questionnaires before two weeks time had elapsed in an effort to avoid measuring a "bubble effect" immediately following conferences. An analysis of time elapsed from disposition to completion of questionnaire failed to detect any relationship to participant responses.

Surveys were mailed and accompanied by a letter signed by the police commissioner and a stamped return envelope addressed to the police liaison officer. To increase the sample size, follow-up phone calls were conducted no sooner than two weeks after the surveys were first sent. When appropriate, survey interviews were conducted over the phone. In several cases where attempts to contact had failed, personal visits were made. Of the 180 victim surveys received, 75 percent were received by mail and 25 percent by phone interview. Of the 233 offender surveys received, 52 percent were received by mail, 45 percent by phone interview, and 3 percent through a personal visit. Of the 169 parent surveys received, 53 percent were received by mail, 45 percent by phone interview, and 2 percent through a personal visit.

The overall survey response rates were 67 percent for victims, 67 percent for offenders, and 54 percent for parents. As shown in Exhibit 32, there were significant differences in response rates, depending on experimental group and crime type. The conference groups had the highest response rates for victims, offenders and parents. This did not remain significant for violent cases, when controlling for crime type. However, it did hold true for property case offenders, parents and victims, $\chi^2(1, n = 148) = 15.6$, $p < .001$, $\chi^2(1, n = 107) = 11.0$, $p < .001$ and $\chi^2(1, n = 117) = 13.3$, $p < .001$, respectively. In violent cases, conferenced offenders and victims did have slightly higher response rates than decline and control group offenders and victims, but these differences were not significant. The response rates for conference, control and decline group parents were virtually identical among violent cases. There were no significant differences in response rates between control and decline groups among offenders, parents or victims.

Exhibit 32
Participant survey response rates

	offenders		parents		victims	
	%	n	%	n	%	n
total	67%	233	54%	169	67%	180
control	63%	83	44%	64	61%	57
conference	84%	80	72%	46	83%	65
decline	51%	70	53%	59	55%	58

Response rates were also compared across a number of other variables. Overall, offenders in retail theft cases were more likely than offenders in other types of cases to respond to the survey, 75 percent versus 61 percent, $\chi^2(1, n = 233) = 4.5$, $p < .05$. Also, parents of offenders who were white were more likely than parents of nonwhite offenders to respond to the survey, 64 percent versus 47 percent, $\chi^2(1, n = 169) = 4.5$, $p < .05$. The difference in response rates between white and nonwhite offenders, 73 percent versus 61 percent, was not quite significant, $\chi^2(1, n = 233) = 3.6$, $p = .056$. There were no overall differences among victims.

Among just the conference group, the race effect was no longer significant for offenders or parents. Offenders who lived in Zip3 were more likely than offenders who lived in other zip codes to respond to the post-conference survey, 100 percent versus 80 percent, $\chi^2(1, n = 80) = 3.9$, $p < .05$. Property offenders were more likely than violent offenders to respond to the survey, 89 percent versus 71 percent, $\chi^2(1, n = 80) = 4.2$, $p < .05$. Also, offenders with no prior arrests were more likely than offenders with at least one prior arrest to respond to the survey, 88 percent versus 64 percent, $\chi^2(1, n = 80) = 4.7$, $p < .05$. Offenders and parents of offenders whose victim was a retail store or an individual were more likely than offenders and parents of offenders whose victim was a school to respond to the survey, for offenders 88 percent versus 50 percent, $\chi^2(1, n = 80) = 7.4$, $p < .01$, for parents 78 percent versus 20 percent, $\chi^2(1, n = 46) = 7.4$, $p < .01$.

Among just the control and decline groups, the race effect remained significant for parents of offenders, $\chi^2(1, n = 123) = 4.1$, $p < .05$, and almost significant for offenders, $\chi^2(1, n = 153) = 3.8$, $p = .053$. That is, parents of white offenders were more likely than parents of nonwhite offenders to respond to the court survey, 59 percent versus 40 percent, and white offenders were more likely than nonwhite offenders to respond to the survey, 66 percent versus 51 percent. Victims of violent crimes were more likely than victims of property crimes to respond to the survey, 72 percent versus 49 percent, $\chi^2(1, n = 115) = 6.5$, $p < .05$. Similarly, individual or school victims were more likely than retail theft victims to respond to the survey, 67 percent versus 47 percent, $\chi^2(1, n = 115) = 4.5$, $p < .05$.

The conference group had the highest response rate for victims, offenders and parents. Among the overall sample of offenders and their parents, white offenders and their parents were over-represented compared to Latino offenders and their parents. Also, property offenders and their parents responding were over-represented compared to violent offenders and their parents. For victims, however, the opposite was true: responding victims of violent crimes were over-represented compared to victims of property crimes. Within the conference group, offenders were more likely to respond if they had no prior arrests and lived in Zip3. Again, we were unable to determine what factors might be involved in differences between zip codes.

This chapter presents the results of the participant surveys for victims, offenders and parents of offenders, summarizing the results and drawing conclusions after each section. Chapter 9 draws these conclusions together and relates them more directly to the hypotheses articulated in Chapter 1.

VICTIM SURVEY RESULTS

Of the total of 180 victims who were sent a survey, 67 percent responded. The highest response was in the conference group with 83 percent ($n = 65$), then the control group with 61 percent ($n = 57$) and the decline group with 55 percent ($n = 58$).

Conference versus Court

Four questions were asked both of victims who attended conferences and victims whose cases were processed by formal adjudication:

1) How satisfied were you with the way your case was handled?
2) Did you experience fairness within the justice system in your case?
3) Was the offender adequately held accountable for the offense committed?
4) Do you feel your opinion regarding the offense and circumstances were adequately considered in this case?

As shown in Exhibit 33, crime victims who participated in a conference were more satisfied with the way their case was handled than those whose cases were processed through court: 96 percent of conference group victims, compared to 79 percent of control group victims and 73 percent of decline group victims, $\chi^2(2, n = 116) = 9.6, p < .01$. Among the court cases, victim satisfaction was not significantly related to the disposition of the offender (handled informally, acquit or guilty).

As shown in Exhibit 34, 96 percent of conferenced victims, 79 percent of the control group victims and 81 percent of the decline group victims said they experienced fairness in the handling of their case. Conferenced victims were more likely than control or decline group victims to experience fairness, $\chi^2(2, n = 112) = 7.1, p < .05$. Crime victims whose offenders had pled guilty in court are generally unaware of the court disposition. In fact, among the court cases, victim experience of fairness was not significantly related to the disposition of the offender. The control and decline group victims were presumably rating the handling of the

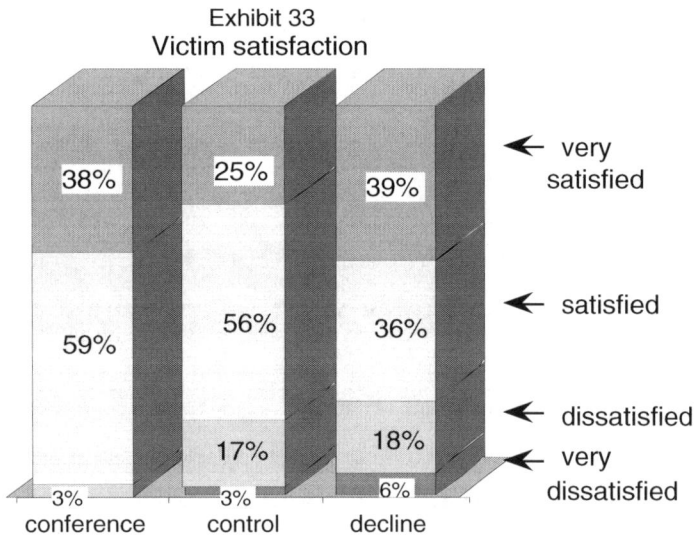

Exhibit 33
Victim satisfaction

case by the police rather than the justice system as a whole. Of course, all conferenced victims knew precisely the outcome of the case as they played a primary role in designing that outcome.

When asked if the offenders had been adequately held accountable, 93 percent of conferenced victims agreed, compared with 74 percent of the control group and 77 percent of the decline group victims as shown in Exhibit 35. These differences were not quite statistically significant, $\chi^2(2, n = 115) = 5.9, p = .053$. Again, for non-conferenced crime victims, the arrest of the offender may be a sufficient sign of offender accountability, even if they do not know the ultimate resolution of the case. This did not appear to be true, however; among the court cases, victims' sense of accountability was significantly related to the disposition of the offender. Victims whose offenders were found guilty were significantly more likely to feel that the offender had been held accountable, 90 percent for guilty dispositions versus 50 percent for other dispositions (does not include cases not yet disposed), $\chi^2(1, n = 59) = 11.5, p < .001$.

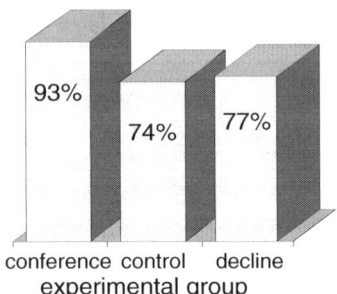

Exhibit 35
Victims agreeing offender was held accountable

Finally, when asked if their opinion was adequately considered, 94 percent of conferenced victims agreed, compared with 91 percent of the control group and 94 percent of the decline group as shown in Exhibit 36. In general, crime victims felt that their opinion had been considered, probably influenced greatly by the fact that police had decided to press formal charges against the offender, since disposition was not significantly related to victims feeling their opinion was considered.

There were no significant differences between the control and treatment (decline and conference combined) victims for the satisfaction, fairness, accountability and opinion items. When controlling for crime type, however, there was a significant difference among victims of property crime. In this subgroup, the treatment group was more likely to say the offender was adequately held accountable for the offense, $\chi^2(1, n = 71) = 4.2, p < .05$.

Within the treatment group, there were significant differences

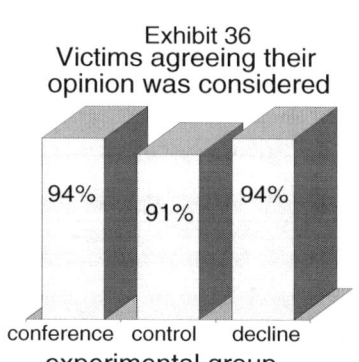

Exhibit 36
Victims agreeing their opinion was considered

between the decline and conference groups. Conferenced victims were more likely than decline group victims to be satisfied with how their case was handled, to experience fairness and to feel the offender was held accountable. Controlling for crime type, the difference in satisfaction rates remained significant for both property crime victims and violent crime victims—$\chi^2(1, n = 52) = 4.3, p < .05$ and $\chi^2(1, n = 31) = 4.3, p < .05$, respectively—but differences in fairness and accountability rates were no longer significant for either crime grouping of victims.

There were significant differences between conferenced victims and a collapsed court group (decline and control combined). Crime victims attending a conference were more likely than court victims to be satisfied with how their case was handled, to experience fairness, and to feel the offender was held accountable. Controlling for crime type, the difference in satisfaction rates remained significant for both property crime victims and violent crime victims—$\chi^2(1, n = 72) = 4.6, p < .05$ and $\chi^2(1, n = 44) = 4.1, p < .05$, respectively—but differences in fairness and accountability rates were no longer significant for either crime grouping of victims.

Court Only

Several questions were asked only of victims whose cases were disposed via the formal adjudication process. As shown in Exhibit 37, 79 percent said they felt a meeting with the offender might be helpful, 23 percent said they had a positive attitude toward the offender, 39 percent said they were no longer upset about the crime, and 74 percent said they were not afraid that the offender would commit another crime against them. There were no significant differences when the group was divided by crime type (violent crime versus property crime) or experimental group (control or decline).

Conference Only

Several questions were asked only of victims who attended family group conferences. As shown in Exhibit 38, 96 percent said they felt that participating in the conference was their own choice; 92 percent said they would recommend conferences to others; 94 percent said they would choose a conference if they had to do it over again; 93 percent said meeting with the offender was helpful; 94 percent said the tone of the conference was

Exhibit 37
Court victims attitudes toward offense and offender

	total		control		decline		property		violent	
	%	n	%	n	%	n	%	n	%	n
meeting offender helpful	79%	62	79%	33	79%	29	81%	32	77%	30
positive toward offender	23%	65	21%	34	26%	31	18%	33	28%	32
no longer upset about crime	39%	64	44%	34	33%	30	39%	33	39%	31
not afraid of reoffense	74%	65	74%	34	74%	31	70%	33	78%	32

basically friendly. Additionally, 96 percent of conferenced victims said the offender apologized; 88 percent said the offender seemed sorry about what he or she did; and 81 percent said they thought conferences should be offered to all victims.

Regarding the tone of the conference, some respondents gave descriptions other than "friendly" or "hostile" including "stressful," "casual and comfortable," "mixed," "business-like," "tense" and "all emotions but mostly embarrassment."

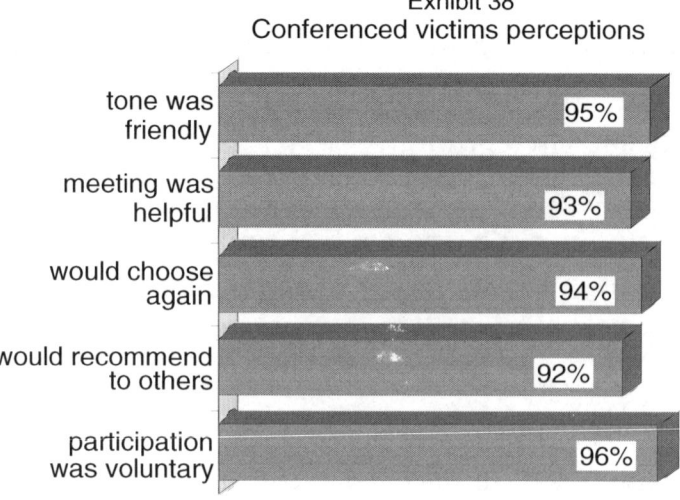

Exhibit 38
Conferenced victims perceptions

A major difference between property and violent crime victims who participated in conferences was that victims of violent crimes were much more likely to have known the offender before the offense than victims of property crimes, $\chi^2 (1, n = 53) = 29.0, p < .001$. In addition, there were slight differences in feeling that participation in the conference was their own choice and the likelihood that the offender apologized, $\chi^2(1, n= 53) = 6.4, p < .05, \chi^2(1, n = 52) = 6.2, p < .05$, respectively; there were two victims of violent crimes who said that participation was not their own choice, and two victims of violent crimes who said that the offender did not apologize (versus no victims of property crimes who said participation was not their own choice and that the offender did not apologize).

Victims who participated in conferences were also asked what the most significant effects of the offense were for them, why they chose to participate in the conference, if they were surprised by anything in the conference, and if so, what surprised them.

The most frequent effect of the offense mentioned by victims was the loss of property ($n = 35$), then damage to property ($n = 7$), a feeling of powerlessness ($n = 6$), the hassle of dealing with police and court officials ($n = 4$), and a greater sense of fear ($n = 3$).

The most frequent reasons given for choosing to participate in the conference were to help the offender ($n = 35$), to tell the offender how they were affected ($n = 21$), to receive an apology ($n = 13$), to receive answers to questions they wanted to ask the offender ($n = 9$), and to get paid pack for their losses ($n = 8$). Other reasons that victims added included "to hold the offender accountable in front of parents" ($n = 2$), "to see the effect of the study" ($n = 2$), "to assist in study to find alternatives in juvenile justice system" ($n = 1$), "to have kids understand what was done was wrong" ($n = 1$), and "I was asked to participate" ($n = 1$).

Of all conferenced victims, 31 percent said they were surprised by something in the conference. The reasons were: "it went better than expected" ($n = 8$), "the offender seemed sincere" ($n = 8$), "the offender was arrogant" ($n = 2$), "it was so friendly" ($n = 1$), "the way the offenders opened up in front of parents" ($n = 1$).

Conferenced victims were asked to say whether they agreed or disagreed with six statements made by victims who have participated in family group conferences. As shown in Exhibit 39, 98 percent agreed that "Family Group Conferencing allowed me to express my feelings about being victimized"; 94 percent agreed that "Conferencing allows for fuller participation in the justice system"; 75 percent disagreed that "The offender's participation was insincere"; 62 percent agreed that "I have a better understanding of why the offense was committed against me"; 56 percent disagreed that "The offender participated only because he/she was trying to avoid punishment"; and 92 percent agreed that "Conferences make the justice process more responsive to my needs as a human being."

When the group was divided by crime type, there were significant differences among two items. Victims of violent crime were more likely to agree that the offender's participation was insincere and that the offender participated only because they were trying to avoid punishment, $\chi^2(1, n=52) = 4.1, p < .05$ and $\chi^2(1, n = 52) = 4.4, p < .05$, respectively.

Exhibit 39
Conferenced victims attitudes toward conferencing

	total % n	violent % n	property % n
Agreed that "Conferencing allowed me to express my feelings about being victimized."	98% 52	100% 13	97% 39
Agreed that "Conferencing allows for fuller participation in the justice system."	94% 51	100% 12	92% 39
Disagreed that "The offender's participation was insincere."	75% 52	54% 13	82% 39
Agreed that "I have a better understanding of why the offense was committed against me."	62% 50	46% 11	67% 39
Disagreed that "The offender participated only because he/she were trying to avoid punishment."	56% 52	31% 13	64% 39
Agreed that "Conferences make the justice process more responsive to my needs as a human being."	92% 52	100% 13	90% 39

Perceptions of Justice and the Justice System

Victims were asked to specify their most important concern about fairness in the justice system, from a list of six items. The top three general concerns about fairness for victims in both the conference and court groups were "helping the offender," "having the offender personally make things right," and "punishing the offender."

Victims were also asked to indicate how important specific items regarding how the case should be handled were to them as shown in Exhibit 40. Of all victims, 80 percent said it was important "to receive answers from the offender"; 89 percent said it was important "to tell the offender how I was affected"; 76 percent said it was important "to get paid back for losses"; 92 percent said it was important "to see that the offender gets counseling or some other type of help"; 80 percent said it was important "to have the offender punished"; 84 percent said it was important "to have the offender say he/she was sorry"; and 73 percent said it was important "to have the opportunity to negotiate a repayment agreement". There were no significant differences between the control and treatment groups.

Among treatment group victims (conference and decline), receiving answers to questions and telling the offender how they were affected was more important for conferenced victims than decline victims. When controlling for crime type, receiving answers to questions and telling the offender how they were affected was significant only among violent crimes victims, $\chi^2(1, n = 30) = 5.1, p < .05$ and $\chi^2(1, n = 31) = 4.9, p < .05$, respectively. Also, among violent crimes victims, helping the offender was more important for decline victims than conferenced victims, $\chi^2(1, n = 29) = 4.1, p < .05$.

Exhibit 40
Importance of issues for victims

	total %	total n	control %	control n	conference %	conference n	decline %	decline n
To receive answers from offender	80%	115	82%	34	87%	52	66%	29
To tell offender how affected	89%	118	85%	34	98%	54	77%	30
To get paid back for losses	76%	111	79%	33	74%	50	75%	28
To see that offender gets help	92%	116	88%	34	91%	53	100%	29
To have offender punished	80%	115	85%	34	72%	54	89%	27
To have offender say sorry	84%	117	82%	34	89%	54	76%	29
To negotiate acceptable agreement	73%	115	77%	34	73%	52	69%	29

When comparing court victims to conferenced victims, telling the offender how they were affected was more important for conferenced victims and having the offender punished was more important for court victims. When controlling for crime type, telling the offender how they were affected was more important for conferenced victims among the violent crime group, $\chi^2(1, n = 45) = 5.1, p < .05$, but not significantly different among the property crimes group. Differences in wanting to have the offender punished were no longer statistically significant. Also, among violent crimes victims, receiving answers to questions was significantly more important for conferenced victims, $\chi^2(1, n = 44) = 4.2, p < .05$.

Additional Comments

Some victims who participated in conferences made additional comments on their surveys. Positive comments generally said the process was helpful and the police handled the case well. One convenience store owner commented:

> The offenders were honest and friendly. They wanted to make things right, which I appreciate. The police department as a whole is very efficient and helpful to everybody, which enables me to say I am impressed by their work. The police officers involved in this case were really working behind getting the offenders on track.

One young victim commented:

> I was really scared but my mom said this is how to do things, because fighting will never get anybody anywhere. It has also helped get the others back to reality. My mom says sometimes there is something missing and they are somehow looking for it and hurt people on the way. My mom also says the conferences are like a push on the right track.

A couple people commented that the process was preferable to court because it helps teach kids right and wrong. For instance, one victim wrote:

> This is an important community service. The children need to be taught what is right and wrong. I think that education is more important than punishment. Educating a person could prevent them from committing crimes by showing them what impact it has on all of us.

Others thought the process went well but were skeptical about the offender's sincerity and commitment not to re-offend. For example:

> I enjoyed taking part in this program! I do not feel that one meeting will change the offender's behavior. It was easy for the offender to predict what we wanted to hear. I'm not sure this program will be successful for all offenders. It's a great start though!

A few victims expressed their concern about follow-up on agreements because they either did not receive their restitution or did not know if the agreement had been carried out yet. A couple of victims commented that there should have been more guidelines for appropriate restitution and community service options. One store manager said:

> My expectations of what the conference was weren't met. I view court as getting out of punishment and thought they would learn a lesson from the conference. I felt more needed to be done. The offenders and their parents were given too much of a say. There were no guidelines—when I said 30 hours of community service, everyone looked at me like I was a monster. I felt my participation didn't mean that much.

One store owner was concerned because he lost the offender's parents as customers, while another retailer commented that the offender's mother was coming to the store again.

There were a couple of comments related to the problem of having English-speaking and non-English-speaking participants in a conference, one that there needed to be an interpreter, another that the interpreter needed to be a neutral individual rather than a family member.

Victims of offenders whose cases were referred to formal adjudication also made comments on their surveys. The most frequent comment was that they did not know what happened to the offender because they were never informed of the hearing or its outcome.

Most positive comments were related to how the police department handled the case. Some examples:

> I have five service stations and convenience stores and have dealt frequently with police departments in Allentown, Palmer and now the new Colonial Police.

> Without question the Bethlehem Police are the most responsive to businessmen's needs and concerns and do the most effective job. I appreciate the job you all are doing!

> The officer was kind, considerate, understanding and very professional.

A few victims expressed dissatisfaction with outcomes. For example:

> I felt I wasn't asked to be involved in the hearing. I thought there should have been community service. He didn't learn a lesson.

> The court costs made the restitution paid inadequate in repairing the store's expenses.

Conclusions

The comparisons of conference versus court show a clear pattern: victims who participated in conferences were more satisfied with how their case was handled, had higher perceptions of fairness, and were more likely to feel the offender was held accountable than victims whose cases went through formal adjudication. While the evidence suggests that the conferencing process was responsible for these more favorable perceptions, the findings are not conclusive, since victims self-selected to participate and reactions were favorable for court-processed victims as well. Nevertheless, conferencing appears to be as good as formal adjudication in facilitating a satisfying experience of justice for victims of lesser juvenile offenses.

The results of the conference-only questions and the additional comments made by victims further illustrates the satisfying experience of justice from conferences. Victim dissatisfaction with conferencing in the two cases related to inadequate follow-up on agreements and the mishandling of conference protocol on the part of the facilitator.

Victims whose cases were processed through formal adjudication also reported satisfying experiences of justice. Comments suggested that dissatisfaction with the court process were related to not knowing about the hearing and not knowing the outcome of the case. Nevertheless, the results suggest that a conference may have been useful for these victims, especially given the large proportion of control and decline group victims who felt a meeting with the offender might be helpful and who had negative feelings about the offense and the offender.

Lastly, restorative responses—such as apologies, reparation, making things right and helping the offender—are equally if not more important than punishment of offenders for victims of juvenile crime.

OFFENDER SURVEY RESULTS

Of the total of 233 offenders who were sent a survey, 67 percent responded. The highest response was in the conference group with 84 percent ($n = 80$), then the control group with 63 percent ($n = 83$) and the decline group with 51 percent ($n = 70$).

Conference versus Court

Four questions were asked both of offenders who participated in conferences and offenders who were referred to formal adjudication:

1) How satisfied were you with the way the justice system handled your case?
2) Did you experience fairness within the justice system in your case?
3) Were you adequately held accountable for the offense you committed?
4) What is your attitude toward the victim?

When asked how satisfied they were with the way their case was handled, 97 percent of the conferenced offenders, 96 percent of the control group, and 86 percent of the decline group said they were satisfied. These differences were not quite significant, $\chi^2(2, n = 145) = 5.6$, $p = .06$. However, as shown in Exhibit 41, conferenced offenders were much more likely to say they were *very* satisfied, with 63 percent reporting that they were very satisfied, compared to 34 percent for the control group and 24 percent for the decline group, $\chi^2(2, n = 145) = 16.9$, $p < .001$. Among the court cases, offender satisfaction was not significantly related to the disposition (handled informally, acquit or guilty).

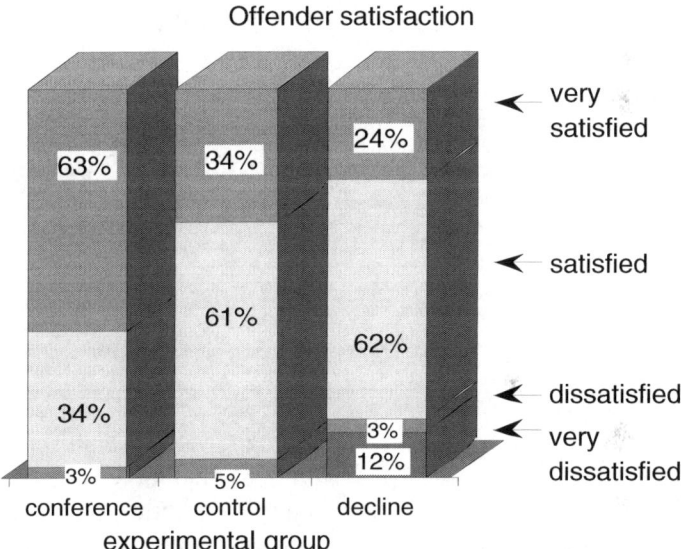

Exhibit 41
Offender satisfaction

Ninety-seven percent of conferenced offenders, 93 percent of the control group, and 79 percent of the decline group said they experienced fairness in their case. These differences were statistically significant, $\chi^2(2, n = 145) = 9.3$, $p < .01$. Among the court cases, offender experience of fairness was not significantly related to the disposition.

Ninety-one percent of conferenced offenders, 82 percent of the control group, and 94 percent of the decline group felt that they had been adequately held accountable. This was not a significant difference. Offenders' sense of their own accountability was unrelated to the court disposition of the case for those cases going through magistrate court.

As shown in Exhibit 42, 80 percent of conferenced offenders, 62 percent of the control group, and 47 percent of the decline group said they had a positive attitude toward the victim.

Conferenced offenders were more likely than court or decline group offenders to have a positive attitude toward the victim, χ^2 (2, $n=141$) = 11.5, $p < .01$.

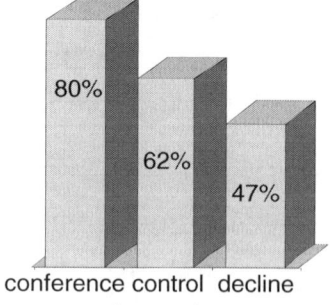

Exhibit 42
Offender attitude toward victim
percent reporting positive attitude

There were no significant differences between the control and treatment groups (combined conference and decline) for any of these four items. When comparing the two treatment groups (decline and conference), three of these four items were significantly different. Conferenced offenders were more likely to say they were satisfied and experienced fairness, and more often had positive attitudes toward their victims. Controlling for crime type, these differences remained significant only for the property offender group, χ^2 (1, $n = 70$) = 4.5, $p < .05$, $\chi^2(1, n = 70) = 10.6$, $p < .01$ and $\chi^2(1, n = 69) = 8.4$, $p < .01$, respectively.

There were significant differences between the conference group and a collapsed court group (decline and control combined). Conferenced offenders were more likely than court offenders to experience fairness and to have a positive attitude toward their victim. Controlling for crime type, these differences remained significant for property cases only, $\chi^2(1, n = 100) = 5.3$, $p < .05$ and $\chi^2(1, n = 99) = 7.9$, $p < .01$, respectively.

Court Only

Several questions were asked only of offenders whose cases were referred to formal adjudication. As shown in Exhibit 43, 75 percent said they thought a meeting with the victim might be helpful; 37 percent had a positive attitude toward meeting the victim; 51 percent said they would be nervous about a meeting attended by the victim and their family and friends; and 43 percent said they cared what the victim thought about them.

Exhibit 43
Court offenders attitudes toward victims
percent agreeing with statement

	total %	n	control %	n	decline %	n	property %	n	person %	n
meeting victim helpful	75%	77	86%	44	61%	33	78%	50	70%	27
positive about meeting victim	37%	76	42%	43	30%	33	40%	50	31%	26
nervous about meeting victim	51%	77	52%	44	49%	33	58%	50	37%	27
care what victim thinks	43%	77	52%	44	30%	33	48%	50	33%	27

The only significant difference between control and decline groups was that the control group was more likely to say that a meeting with the victim might be helpful. When controlling for crime type, this remained a significant difference for the property offender group, $\chi^2(1, n = 50) = 6.3$, $p < .05$, but not for the violent offender group. This would be expected given that the decline group is comprised mostly of offenders who had already declined to participate in a conference with their victims. In addition, among property offenders only, control group offenders were more likely than decline group offenders to care what the victim thinks about them, $\chi^2(1, n = 50) = 4.3$, $p < .05$. Among the combined court group (control and decline), there were no significant differences between the property and violent offender groups.

Conference Only

Several questions were asked only of offenders who participated in family group conferences. As shown in Exhibit 44, 92 percent indicated that it was their own choice to participate in the conference; 92 percent said they would recommend conferencing to others who faced similar trouble; 94 percent said if they had to do it over again, they would choose to participate in a conference; all said that meeting with the victim was helpful; 96 percent said the tone of the conference was friendly. Additionally, 95 percent said they apologized to the victim; 80 percent had a positive attitude toward the conference; 92 percent said they thought the victim had a better opinion of them after the conference; and 89 percent said they thought their family had a better opinion of them after the conference.

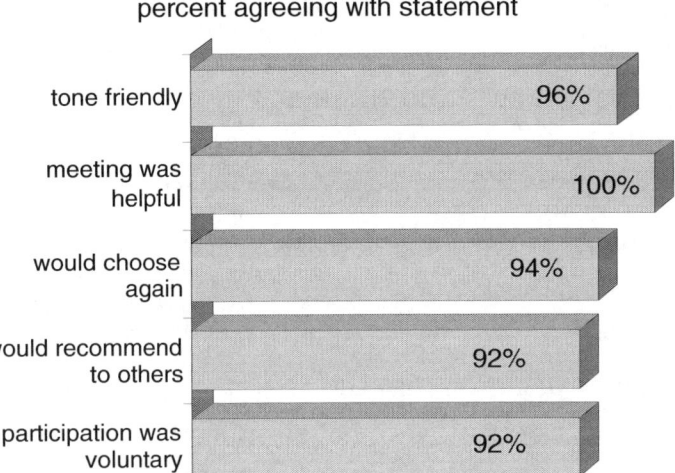

Exhibit 44
Conference offenders perceptions toward conferencing
percent agreeing with statement

Some respondents wrote in descriptions other than "friendly" or "hostile" regarding the tone of the conference, including "mixed," "professional" and "hostile then friendly." Property offenders were more likely than violent offenders to think that their family had a better opinion of them after the conference, $\chi^2(1, n = 61) = 3.9, p < .05$. All other differences between crime types were not statistically significant.

Offenders who participated in conferences were also asked why they chose to participate in the conference, if they were surprised by anything in the conference, and if so, what surprised them. The reasons given for choosing to participate in the conference were to offer an apology ($n = 32$), to make things right ($n = 30$), to let the victim know why they did it ($n = 13$), to help the victim ($n = 5$), and to pay back the victim ($n = 3$). Other reasons given included "to avoid going to the magistrate" ($n = 3$), "I didn't want to pay them back" ($n = 2$) and "to get out of trouble" ($n = 1$).

Forty-eight percent of conferenced offenders were surprised by something that occurred in the conference. The reasons were: "it went better than expected" ($n = 20$), "the victim seemed to care about me" ($n = 11$), "how much I affected people" ($n = 2$), "I found out she lied" ($n = 1$), "the victim was so angry" ($n = 1$), and "it went worse than expected" ($n = 1$).

Conferenced offenders were asked to say whether they agreed or disagreed with seven statements made by offenders who had participated in family group conferences. As shown in Exhibit 45, 77 percent disagreed that "Too much pressure was put on me to do all the talking in the conference"; 81 percent disagreed that "I had no choice about participating in the conference"; 76 percent disagreed that "The victim's participation was insincere"; 76 percent disagreed that "The victim participated only because he/she wanted the money back or to be paid for damages"; 94 percent agreed that "I have a better understanding of how my behavior affected the victim"; 92 percent agreed that "Conferences are more responsive to my needs as a human being"; and 87 percent agreed that "Without Family Group Conferences I probably would have gotten punished much worse." Property offenders were more likely to disagree that the victim's participation was insincere, $\chi^2 (2, n = 63) = 9.5, p < .01$. All other differences were not significant by crime type.

Exhibit 45
Conferenced offenders attitudes toward conferencing

	total %	n	violent %	n	property %	n
Disagreed that "Too much pressure was put on me to do all the talking in the conference."	77%	64	80%	15	76%	49
Disagreed that "I had no choice about participating in the conference."	81%	62	80%	15	81%	47
Disagreed that "The victim's participation was insincere."	76%	63	47%	15	85%	48
Disagreed that "The victim participated only because he/she wanted the money back or to be paid for damages."	76%	63	79%	14	76%	49
Agreed that "I have a better understanding of how my behavior affected the victim."	94%	65	94%	16	94%	49
Agreed that "Conferences are more responsive to my needs as a human being."	92%	63	87%	15	94%	48
Agreed that "Without Family Group Conferences, I would have gotten punished much worse."	87%	63	73%	15	92%	48

Perceptions of Justice and the Justice System

Offenders were asked to specify their most important concern about fairness in the justice system, from a list of six items. The top three general concerns about fairness for offenders in both the conference and court groups were "allowing the offender to apologize to the victim," "having the offender personally make things right," and "paying back the victim."

As shown in Exhibit 46, offenders were also asked to indicate the importance of specific items regarding how their case could be handled. Of all offenders, 92 percent thought it was important "to be able to tell the victim what happened"; 87 percent thought it was important "to compensate the victim by paying money or doing work"; 93 percent thought it was important "to be able to apologize to the victim"; and 96 percent thought it was important "to have the opportunity to negotiate a repayment agreement."

The only significant differences between control and treatment groups were among property offenders only. Treatment group offenders rated the importance

Exhibit 46
Importance of issues for offenders
percent agreeing issue important

	total %	n	control %	n	conference %	n	decline %	n
To be able to tell victim what happened	92%	146	91%	46	94%	67	88%	33
To compensate victim by paying money or doing work	87%	141	89%	45	89%	63	79%	33
To be able to apologize to victim	93%	145	91%	46	97%	66	88%	33
To have opportunity to negotiate repayment agreement	96%	145	94%	46	99%	66	94%	33

of apologizing to the victim slightly higher than control group offenders, $\chi^2(1, n = 99) = 3.9, p < .05$. There were no significant differences between the two treatment groups, decline and conference. The only significant differences between court and conference groups were again among property offenders only. Conference group offenders rated the importance of apologizing to the victim slightly higher than court group offenders, $\chi^2(1, n = 99) = 4.1, p < .05$.

Additional Comments

Some offenders who participated in conferences made comments on their surveys. These comments were generally positive statements about the conferences and with how the case was handled, sometimes expressing thanks to the police department and further apology for the offense. Some examples:

> It's a good program for you to keep alive and I believe that it would help others in the future.

> The conference was good. It was fair. Thank you for letting me participate in the program.

> Well I would like to say that these conferences are good. It brings out everyone's feelings. So I think they are helpful, and thank you for helping me put the conference together.

> I really liked the chance it gave me to apologize and also gave me a wake-up call with minimal punishment.

> I just want to say I really am sorry I committed a stupid mistake and I wish this wouldn't go on my record, because I believe everyone deserves a second chance because no on is perfect!

The one negative comment related to the officer conducting the conference:

> I think we should have a younger and more understanding officer.

Some offenders referred to formal adjudication made comments on their surveys as well, about evenly positive and negative. Some offenders expressed that they were treated fairly, that the case was handled well, that the police did a good job, and that they were remorseful for what they had done. Some examples:

> I was treated adequately and fairly. It's a good system and I am really very sorry that I was caught up in it. I wish to thank the officer for all he did for me.

> I think it was right for them to make me accountable for my actions and not my mom. I think that the magistrate was very fair with my case.

> I feel that the punishment fit the crime. I think that I speak for all of us who took part in this that it was foolish and we regret it.

Other offenders had a more negative view of how the case was handled. A few thought that it was unfair that they were attributed full responsibility for the offense when others played a part. For example, one offender said:

> I understand what I did was wrong and I now regret the actions I made, but the victim had a very big part in this problem and she did not receive any punishment or suspension.

A number of offenders complained about how the police, the court, and store security officers handled the matter. Some examples:

> They treated my mother badly. They screamed at and embarrassed her.

> The guy from the store lied his ass off. The judge is a prick and didn't want to hear what we had to say.

> The police officer lied to us. Our lawyers were good.

Conclusions

Offenders who participated in conferences were more satisfied with how their case was handled, had higher perceptions of fairness, and had substantially more positive attitudes toward their victims than offenders who went through formal adjudication. This suggests, but does not conclusively prove, that conferences help produce more satisfying experiences of justice for offenders than formal adjudication processes, which was further supported by the results of the conference-only questions. It should be noted that all offenders in the study had considerably high levels of satisfaction and perceptions of fairness, regardless of method of disposition.

Conferenced offenders reported that participating in the conference was more favorable than going to court. Most reported that apology and reparation to victims and being held accountable was an important part of the justice process. Most offenders reported they would have gotten punished worse without the conference. Their responses also confirmed the reintegrative quality of conferences; most conferenced offenders indicated that they thought their family and the victim had a better opinion of them after the conference.

A substantial proportion of court-processed offenders said they thought a meeting with the victim might be helpful. It also appeared that more court-processed offenders had lingering resentments about how they were treated by the justice system.

PARENT SURVEY RESULTS

Of the total of 169 parents of offenders who were sent a survey, 67 percent responded. The highest response was in the conference group with 72 percent ($n = 46$), then the decline group with 53 percent ($n = 59$) and the control group with 44 percent ($n = 64$).

Conference versus Court

Eleven questions were asked of both parents of offenders whose cases were referred to court and parents of offenders who cases were conferenced:

1) How satisfied were you with the way the justice system handled your case?
2) Did you experience fairness within the justice system in your case?
3) Do you believe your child was adequately held accountable for the offense committed?
4) Did you feel your opinion regarding the offense and circumstances was adequately considered in this case?
5) How likely is it that your child will commit another similar offense?
6) Was the payment or community service agreement fair to you?
7) Was the payment or community service agreement fair to the victim?
8) Was the payment or community service agreement fair to your child?
9) What is your attitude toward your child now?
10) Do you have a better opinion of your child now?
11) Does the victim have a better opinion of your child now?

As shown in Exhibit 47, 97 percent of the conference group, 93 percent of the control group, and 80 percent of the decline group said they were satisfied with how the justice system handled their case. As with their children, parents were much more likely to say they were *very* satisfied with the conference compared to the control or decline group parents, $\chi^2(2, n = 95) = 11.9, p < .01$. Satisfaction among parents of youth whose cases were formally adjudicated was unrelated to the case outcome for their child (guilty or not).

As shown in Exhibit 48, 97 percent of the conference group, 87 percent of the control group, and 72 percent of the decline group of parents said they experienced fairness, $\chi^2(2, n = 88) = 8.4, p < .05$. Parents of conferenced youth were more likely to report fairness in their child's case than those disposed by courts. Still, a majority of all parents in our survey experienced fairness at the handling of their child's case. Experience of fairness among parents of youth whose cases were formally adjudicated was unrelated to the case outcome for their child (guilty or not).

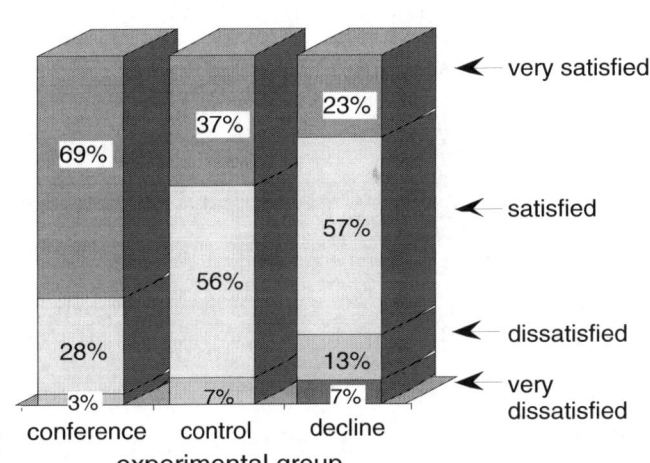

Exhibit 47
Offender's parent satisfaction

Exhibit 48
Offender parents reporting sense of fairness

When asked if the payment or community service agreement from court/conference was fair to themselves, their child, and the victim(s), most parents agreed with all three regardless of how the case was processed. Asked about fairness to themselves, 93 percent of the conferenced parents, 88 percent of the control group parents, and 64 percent of the decline group parents said the outcome was fair to them, $\chi^2(2, n=67) = 7.8, p < .05$. When asked about fairness to the victim, 97 percent of the conferenced parents, 92 percent of the control group parents, and 86 percent of the decline group parents reported the outcome was fair to the victim. Finally, asked about fairness to their child, most parents agreed regardless of how the case was handled: 97 percent of the conferenced parents, all of the control group parents, and 68 percent of the decline group parents reported the outcome was fair to their child. These differences were statistically significant, $\chi^2(2, n=68) = 12.7, p < .01$.

Parents of conferenced offenders were more likely to agree that their child had been adequately held accountable: 94 percent of conferenced parents, 92 percent of control group parents, and 83 percent of the decline group parents felt their child had been adequately held accountable. These differences are not statistically significant, but it is clear that the parents of most offenders in this study felt their child had been held accountable. Sense of accountability among parents of youth whose cases were formally adjudicated was unrelated to the case outcome for their child (guilty or not).

As shown in Exhibit 49, conferenced parents were more likely to have felt their opinion had been adequately considered in their child's case than court-disposed parents. Ninety-two percent of the conference group, 84 percent of the control group, and 55 percent of the decline group parents felt was their opinion was adequately considered, $\chi^2(2, n=90) = 13.2, p < .01$. Feelings about whether their opinions were considered among parents of youth whose cases were formally adjudicated was unrelated to the case outcome for their child (guilty or not).

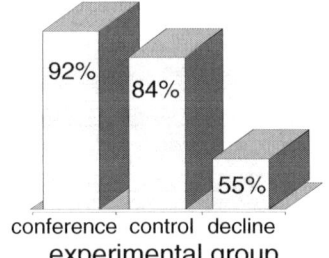

Exhibit 49
Offender parents agreeing their opinion was considered

Although other differences between groups of parents were not statistically significant, the results of questions asked broken down by experimental group of parent were:

86 percent of the conferenced parents, 92 percent of the control group, and 86 percent of the decline group said their child was unlikely to re-offend;

81 percent of the conferenced parents, 78 percent of the control group parents, and 83 percent of the decline group parents said they had a positive attitude toward their child now;

89 percent of the conferenced parents, 82 percent of the control group, and 88 percent of the decline group reported they had a better opinion of their child now;

82 percent of the conferenced parents, 65 percent of the control group, and 48 percent of the decline group reported they thought the victim had a better opinion of their child now.

There were no statistically significant differences between the control and treatment groups. When comparing the two treatment groups (decline and conference), 6 of these 11 items were significantly different. Parents of conferenced offenders were more likely to be satisfied with how their case was handled, to experience fairness, to feel their opinion was considered, to say the payment or community service agreement was fair to them, to say the payment or community service agreement was fair to their child, and to think the victim had a better opinion of their child now.

Controlling for crime type, satisfaction and experience of fairness were no longer significantly different. Feeling that their opinion was considered remained significantly higher only among parents of violent offenders, $\chi^2(1, n=25) = 6.6, p < .05$. Saying the payment or community service agreement was fair to them and saying the payment or community service agreement was fair to their child was significantly higher only among parents of property offenders, $\chi^2(1, n=38) = 4.1, p < .05$ and $\chi^2(1, n=38) = 3.9, p < .05$, respectively. Thinking the victim had a better of their child now was significantly greater among parents of both property and violent offenders, $\chi^2(1, n=35) = 4.7, p < .05$ and $\chi^2(1, n=20) = 4.6, p < .05$, respectively.

When comparing the collapsed court group (control and decline) with the conference group, 4 of the 11 items were significantly different. Parents of conferenced offenders were more likely to experience fairness, to feel their opinion was considered, to say the payment or community service agreement was fair to them, and to think the victim had a better opinion of their child now.

Only feeling their opinion was considered and thinking the victim had a better opinion remained significant when controlling for crime type, and only among parents of violent offenders, $\chi^2(1, n=34) = 4.4, p < .05$ and $\chi^2(1, n=26) = 4.3, p < .05$, respectively.

Court Only

Several items were only asked of parents of offenders whose cases were referred to formal adjudication, including:

1) Do you think a meeting with the victim might be helpful?
2) What is your attitude toward the idea of meeting with the victim?
3) What is your attitude toward the victim now?
4) Would you be nervous about a meeting with the victim attend by your child, friends and family?

Fifty-five percent of the parents of these offenders reported they thought a meeting with the victim might be helpful; 50 percent said they had a positive attitude toward the idea of meeting with the victim; 53 percent said they had a positive attitude toward the victim; and 26 percent said they would be nervous about meeting with the victim. There were no significant differences between the control and decline groups or by crime type.

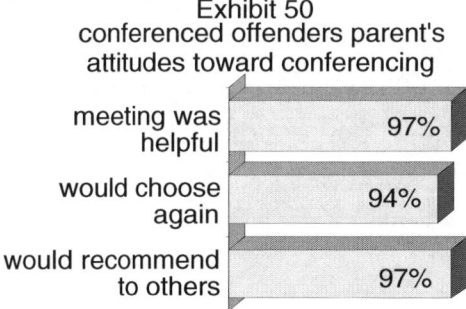

Exhibit 50
conferenced offenders parent's attitudes toward conferencing

meeting was helpful 97%
would choose again 94%
would recommend to others 97%

percent agreeing with statement

When comparing the parents of violent offenders to parents of property offenders combining the control and decline groups, the violent crime group was more likely than the property crime group to believe that a meeting with the victim would be helpful, $\chi^2(1, n = 49) = 5.0$, $p < .05$. Also, the parents of property offenders were over twice as likely to have a positive attitude toward the victim, $\chi^2(1, n = 47) = 6.0$, $p < .05$.

Exhibit 51
Offender's parents perceptions of conferencing

	total		violent		property	
	%	n	%	n	%	n
Agree that "Conferences are more responsive to my needs as a human being"	97%	35	100%	8	96%	27
Agree that "I have a better understanding of how my child's behavior affected the victim"	100%	31	100%	6	100%	25
Agree that "My child was treated with respect in the conference"	100%	35	100%	8	100%	27
Agree that "Without conferences my child would have been punished much worse"	85%	33	100%	8	80%	25
Disagree that "The victim participated only because he/she wanted to be paid for damages"	75%	32	100%	6	69%	26
Disagree that "The victim's participation was insincere"	77%	34	71%	7	78%	27
Disagree that "Too much pressure was put on my child to do all the talking"	91%	34	86%	7	93%	27

Conference Only

Several questions were asked only of parents of offenders who went through family group conferences. As shown in Exhibit 50, nearly all parents of conferenced offenders said they would recommend conferencing to others (97 percent), they would choose to participate in a conference if they had to do it over again (94 percent), they thought that meeting the victim was helpful (97 percent), and they had a positive or very positive attitude toward the conference (91 percent). There were no significant differences between parents of property or violent offenders.

Parents of conferenced offenders were asked to say whether they agreed or disagreed with seven statements made by parents of offenders who participated in family group conferences. As shown in Exhibit 51, 97 percent agreed that "Conferences make the justice process more responsive to my needs as a human being"; all parents agreed that "I have a better understanding of how my child's behavior affected the victim"; all parents agreed that "My child was treated with respect during the conference"; 85 percent agreed that "Without Family Group Conferences my child probably would have gotten punished much worse"; 75 percent disagreed that "The victim participated only because they wanted the money back or to be paid for damages"; 77 percent disagreed that "The victim's participation was insincere"; and 91 percent disagreed that "Too much pressure was put on my child to do all the talking in the conference." There were no significant differences between property and violent crime groups.

Among parents of conferenced offenders, 44 percent said something surprised them about the conference. They were surprised that "it went better than expected" ($n = 11$) and that "the victim seemed to care about my child" ($n = 8$). Other reasons given for being surprised were "my child realized the harm caused" ($n = 1$), "they weren't hard enough on my child" ($n = 1$), "my child's police record was eliminated" ($n = 1$), and "the police were very compassionate" ($n = 1$).

Perceptions of Justice and the Justice System

Parents were asked to specify their most important concern about fairness in the justice system, from a list of six items. The top three general concerns about fairness for parents of offenders in both the conference group and court group were "allowing the offender to apologize to the victim," "having the offender personally make things right," and "paying back the victim."

Parents of offenders were also asked to indicate how important specific items regarding how the case should be handled were to them. As shown in Exhibit 52, 88 percent thought it was important "to tell the victim how I felt"; 99 percent thought it was important "to tell my child how they felt"; 96 percent thought it was important "to have my child apologize to the victim"; 92 percent thought it was important "to apologize for what my child did"; and 96 percent thought it was important "to have the opportunity to negotiate a repayment agreement." There were no significant differences between control and treatment groups.

Exhibit 52
Importance of issues for offender parents
percent agreeing issue important

	total		control		conference		decline	
	%	n	%	n	%	n	%	n
To tell the victim how felt	88%	90	88%	25	94%	36	79%	29
To tell child how felt	99%	92	100%	27	97%	35	100%	30
To have child apologize	96%	92	100%	27	97%	36	90%	29
To apologize for what child did	92%	90	92%	25	100%	36	83%	29
To negotiate repayment agreement	96%	90	92%	25	97%	36	97%	29

Comparing conference and decline groups, the conference group was more likely to indicate it was important to be able to apologize for what their child did. Controlling for crime type, this remained significant only among parents of property offenders, $\chi^2(1, n = 41) = 7.0$, $p < .01$. Also, among parents of property offenders, those whose children attended conferences were more likely to indicate it was important for them to be able to tell the victim how they felt, $\chi^2(1, n = 41) = 6.1$, $p < .05$.

Comparing court and conference groups, the conference group was more likely to indicate it was important to be able to apologize for what their child did. Controlling for crime type, this remained significant only among parents of property offenders, $\chi^2(1, n = 57) = 5.3$, $p < .05$. Also among parents of property offenders, those whose children attended conferences were more likely to indicate it was important for them to be able to tell the victim how they felt, $\chi^2(1, n = 57) = 3.9$, $p < .05$.

Additional Comments

Most of the comments written on surveys came from parents of offenders. On the conference surveys, most of these comments were very positive. Parents said that the conferences went very well and that it was a great learning experience for their child. Here are a few examples:

> I think it is a great idea. I think her being fined and having to face the District Magistrate would be a little too harsh. Thanks to the Family Conference we found out exactly what happened and knew it would never happen again. My daughter suffered enough.

> I'm glad it was handled in a conference instead of going through the system. I think my son has a lot more respect for police because they listened to different sides of the story.

> I was very pleased at how this whole situation was handled. My son learned some very important things. One being that he is held responsible for his actions. Second was that people are forgiving if you are truly sorry for your actions. Having to look someone in the eye and apologize for hurting them and their family taught my son what the consequences are for irresponsible behavior. He learned a valuable lesson that just paying a fine could never have taught him.

> It was great that they had the victim there. It wasn't as easy as my daughter thought it would be. The police officer did a great job. The girls were really sweating it. I'm glad there was a little scare to it.

> It was helpful to me and my child. I wanted to tell her how I feel with other "productive members of society" around me. The conference gave me that chance.

> I feel positive about the whole event. It was part of a learning process for my child. She learned she can't get away with it. The conference drove the points home. It brought the family together around the incident and my child had to be accountable in front of people she didn't know.

There were a few negative comments, mostly related to how the police handled the arrest and what their child's behavior was like after the conference:

> If a child were really sorry for their actions, the Family Group Conference would be of great help in allowing the child and his family to apologize to the victims. My son could care less! He loves the community service—when he attends—and he likes the fact it puts more pressure on me.

> It was a positive experience, but the follow-up community service is not demanding enough. He has yet to tour the prison also.

> The arresting officer was rude. My son didn't deserve that kind of treatment from the officer.

> The conference should have taken more time. My child should have had to talk more. Also, these conferences should only be a one-time thing.

Parents whose children went through formal adjudication also made comments on their surveys. A few wished their case had gone into the conferencing program. For example:

> The officer did a very good, fair, stern job in his interview with my son. He was also very supportive to me the night he had to inform me of the offense. The only problem I have is that my son was put in a position to decide on a meeting with the victim. It was to have happened, didn't and then it took a lot of time to get everything settled.

We felt that our son should have had the opportunity to apologize in person. This was discussed with the police and we were told that the victim's family wouldn't allow it.

There were several statements commenting on how well the magistrate and the police handled the case. For example:

I liked that the magistrate asked both sides if they were happy with the judgment he gave. He made my child agree to write an essay and to bring in her report card to make sure she was doing well in school. He didn't make me pay a fine because I didn't do it. This way she will think twice about what she does next time. There should be more like this magistrate. Thank God for him.

I thought it was excellent. The boys were held accountable, had to see the magistrate two times. Through the experience they had to examine the seriousness of their actions and what could have happened. I truly believe they will think before committing mischievous acts again. I'm grateful that their records are not blemished by this foolishness, but that they had to constructively deal with some consequences of their actions.

I feel the officer was quite professional, and the magistrate attentive, involved and fair. I'm confident the boys learned from the experience and all felt fairly treated.

There were also several statements criticizing how the police, the magistrate and story security handled the case. For example:

Cuffing a 16 year old and taking him to headquarters without reading him his rights is abusive. The arresting officer needs to be watched.

I didn't like the attitude of the police officer. That made me more upset than anything. People from the store said he stole stuff that he didn't steal. The policeman lectured the kid like he was an adult, not a child, which was very disrespectful. We are Hispanic and I sensed prejudice from the officer. I just wanted to get it over with.

We were treated rudely by the security and the police. This wasn't handled in the proper way, especially for first-time stealing. It would have been better to make the child do work, rather than have them arrested and make a big issue out of it. It was a waste of money and it didn't teach them not to do it again.

It was handled like it wasn't a big deal, but to me it was a big deal. He only got a slap on the wrist.

I think everyone should have an opportunity to say something and express their opinion on what happened. All the facts should be put on the table. I was most upset with the officer's attitude toward me in front of my children. It was terrible.

I wish I would have known the case was dropped. The complainant's family moved. I wished we would have been told formally that the charges were dropped. I think my son did learn a lesson from being arrested and was held accountable.

Conclusions

Again, all parents of offenders in the study, including those whose cases went through formal adjudication, had high rates of satisfaction and perceptions of fairness. Nevertheless, parents of offenders who participated in conferences had higher rates of satisfaction and perceptions of fairness than parents of court-processed offenses. Also, parents of conferenced offenders were more likely to feel their opinion was considered and that the victim had a better opinion of their child now.

Parents consistently showed positive perceptions of and attitudes toward conferences. They reported that the conference was beneficial to their child as well as to themselves, and appreciated the opportunity for their child to learn a lesson and for them to tell the victim how they felt about what happened. A few parents, however, did indicate that the conference did not hold their child accountable enough.

The results suggest that parents of court-processed offenders would have benefited by a conference. Over half thought that meeting with the victim would be helpful and had positive attitudes toward the victim and the idea of meeting with the victim. Some of the comments also illustrated that parents would have liked a chance for their child to meet the victim and apologize. Overall, parents reported that punishment of offenders was less important than apology, reparation and making things right.

6
Recidivism

Restorative justice is a new paradigm of justice. Evaluating a new paradigm by the criteria of the old paradigms is inappropriate. While reduction in recidivism is not the central goal of restorative justice, neither is it irrelevant to the paradigm. The goals of restorative justice are to meet the real needs of victims, offenders, and their communities created by the criminal act. Offenders are expected to be held accountable for the consequences of their misbehavior, as a way to begin to address the offender's need to learn responsible behavior. Holding offenders accountable in a reintegrative manner is expected to affect their future behavior, but changing that behavior is not the primary purpose of restoration.

Crime victims need to have their injuries acknowledged and to be reassured that the offenses was not their fault. They need to feel a restoration of safety and to know that something is being done to address their needs. Victim surveys have demonstrated that one of the primary reasons for victims to report crimes to the police is to prevent the future victimization of themselves or others by the offender (Karmen, 1990, p.166, citing National Crime Survey). To the degree that restorative processes are able to address this need, offender recidivism is important for crime victims.

Communities need to know that hurtful behavior will not be tolerated and that concrete measures are being taken to hold offenders accountable to help prevent a reoccurrence of the offense. Thus, reducing offender recidivism is one measure of the capacity of restorative approaches to address the important needs created by a criminal offense. A reduction in reoffending is not the primary purpose, as in deterrence theory, but is one of a number of important goals for the restorative approach to crime. It is assumed that holding offenders accountable to their victims to repair the harm caused should increase offender empathy and thereby lead to a reduction in offending behavior. Thus, recidivism reduction might be considered a secondary goal of restorative justice.

A standard measure of a program's success has been to compare the recidivism rates of offenders receiving the program with offenders not receiving the program. A program's effect of reducing reoffenses is taken as a central measure of success. Certainly, for programs operating from within a deterrence perspective, recidivism is a make-or-break test of program success. This is as it should be for punitive responses to crime since the only justification for inflicting the social "evil" of punishment on the offender is that it will produce the greater good of fewer crimes (specific and/or general deterrence). This was Bentham's justification for punishment, the utilitarian calculus. Thus, from a deterrent perspective punitive programs that cannot demonstrate a reduction in offending have failed to meet the justification for punishment.

However, programs which clearly do not reduce recidivism are often continued. If they cannot demonstrate a deterrent effect, then they may be justified based upon a "just desert" theory of punishment. Thus, punitive approaches become justified, even when they fail to deter, because punitive approaches often resort to multiple goals, with retribution as the last justification for otherwise failing programs. Under a desert theory, a program may still be considered a success even if it is demonstrated that recidivism is higher for those offenders involved—if the punishment was in proportion to the offense, because that punishment would be seen as fair and deserved.

Restorative justice rejects both rationales for punishment and, therefore, cannot fall back on a desert justification should the programs fail to reduce recidivism. Even if recidivism is not reduced, restorative approaches could be justified if they significantly meet other needs of victims, offenders and their communities. This is not a change in justification, but is consistent with the paradigm's priority of goals (McCold, 1997). If it were demonstrated that a restorative program increased reoffending, then it could not be justified as it would fail to meet the restorative purpose, because it would increase rather than reduce the needs of victims, offenders and communities. Thus, restorative justice attempts to balance the needs of victim, offender and communities rather than being solely offender-focused as are the punishment theories of justice.

Reduction in recidivism is central to deterrence-based approaches, central to rehabilitative approaches, and central to incapacitative approaches (at least for the period of incapacitation). Reduction in recidivism is irrelevant to pure desert-based approaches since appropriate punishment is not seen as a social evil but as a positive good. Reduction in recidivism is important, but is not central to the practice of restorative justice. Still, restorative programs which reduce recidivism are to be preferred over programs which have no measurable effect on recidivism. Only restorative programs which tend to increase reoffending would be considered failures from within the paradigm.

Methods

In this study a recidivist event is defined as a rearrest by the Bethlehem Police Department. Each offender included in the study was tracked for rearrests for up to 12 months following the precipitating arrest event, or through the end of October 1997. The number of offenders rearrested was calculated at 30-day intervals and at the one-year point. More recently processed cases whose rearrest follow-up period is shorter than earlier cases censors the number of valid cases, thus decreasing the denominator during the later months. It is possible for the cumulative rates to decrease since the number of cases included in the follow-up period may decrease independent of the number of recidivism events. The cumulative recidivism rates were calculated using the number of valid "noncensored" cases at each point.

There are four possible hypotheses about recidivism:

1) No treatment or self-selection effect
2) Self-selection effect, but no treatment effect
3) Treatment effect, but no self-selection effect
4) Treatment and a self-selection effect

If there was no treatment effect or self-selection effect (hypothesis #1), control, decline and conference groups would all have the same recidivism rates. If there was a self-selection effect, but no treatment effect (hypothesis #2), the conference group should have a lower recidivism rate than the decline group, because "higher-risk offenders" are less likely to participate in conferences. The control group recidivism rate should be exactly between the conference and decline groups.

If there were a treatment effect but no self-selection effect (hypothesis #3), the conference group would have the lowest recidivism rate and control and decline groups would be equal. If there were a treatment effect and a self-selection effect (hypothesis #4), the pattern would be similar to that under hypothesis #2, but the control group rate would be closer to the decline group rate than the conference group rate.

Results

The cumulative recidivism rates are shown in Exhibit 53. There is a statistical problem with the small number of cases recidivating by 12 months. For example, 4 of the 20 (20 percent) violent conferenced offenders have been rearrested at least once since their precipitating arrest compared to 9 of the 26 (35 percent) violent control group offenders. All four conferenced recidivists were rearrested within 6 months and the apparent rate increase from 17 percent to 20 percent after 6 months is not due to an increased number of recidivist events, but only to a smaller number of uncensored cases in the denominator, unlike the violent controls and declines.

Differences must be huge to be statistically significant

Exhibit 53a
Rearrest rates by days of exposure
for violent offenders

days of exposure	control			treatment			conference			decline		
	% of Valid N	# rearrested	Valid N	% of Valid N	# rearrested	Valid N	% of Valid N	# rearrested	Valid N	% of Valid N	# rearrested	Valid N
30	9%	3	35	5%	4	76	0%	0	24	8%	4	52
60	11%	4	35	13%	10	76	4%	1	24	17%	9	52
90	14%	5	35	18%	14	76	8%	2	24	23%	12	52
120	14%	5	35	20%	15	76	13%	3	24	23%	12	52
150	17%	6	35	20%	15	76	13%	3	24	23%	12	52
180	18%	6	33	24%	18	76	17%	4	24	27%	14	52
210	19%	6	31	28%	21	75	17%	4	24	33%	17	51
240	26%	7	27	30%	21	71	17%	4	24	36%	17	47
270	31%	8	26	34%	20	59	18%	4	22	43%	16	37
300	31%	8	26	34%	20	58	18%	4	22	44%	16	36
330	35%	9	26	34%	20	58	18%	4	22	44%	16	36
360	35%	9	26	37%	20	54	19%	4	21	48%	16	33
365	35%	9	26	38%	20	53	20%	4	20	48%	16	33

Exhibit 53b
Rearrest rates by days of exposure for property offenders

days of exposure	control			treatment			conference			decline		
	% of Valid N	# rearrested	Valid N	% of Valid N	# rearrested	Valid N	% of Valid N	# rearrested	Valid N	% of Valid N	# rearrested	Valid N
30	0%	0	68	7%	8	113	0%	0	56	14%	8	57
60	0%	0	68	12%	13	113	7%	4	56	16%	9	57
90	3%	2	68	13%	15	113	7%	4	56	19%	11	57
120	6%	4	68	14%	16	113	7%	4	56	21%	12	57
150	6%	4	68	17%	19	113	11%	6	56	23%	13	57
180	11%	7	64	20%	22	112	14%	8	56	25%	14	56
210	11%	7	63	23%	24	106	18%	10	56	28%	14	50
240	16%	9	56	27%	28	104	21%	12	56	33%	16	48
270	16%	9	56	29%	28	97	24%	12	51	35%	16	46
300	19%	10	54	31%	29	94	26%	13	50	36%	16	44
330	19%	10	53	31%	29	94	26%	13	50	36%	16	44
360	21%	11	53	33%	30	90	32%	15	47	35%	15	43
365	21%	11	53	33%	30	90	32%	15	47	35%	15	43

with this small a sample size, and caution should be exercised in generalizing the results. However, even with the small numbers of cases in the study, conferenced violent offenders were significantly less likely to be rearrested in a 12-month period than violent offenders whose cases were unable to be conferenced, $\chi^2(1, n = 90) = 4.3$, $p < .05$. Differences in the recidivism rates of property offenders is statistically negligible.

The findings for violent offenders illustrated in Exhibit 54a support the hypothesis that there was a self-selection effect, but no treatment effect (hypothesis #2). Violent offenders participating in conferences had significantly lower 12-month rearrest rates than those who were referred to a conference but did not participate. However, the control group rearrest rate is almost exactly between the decline and conference group rearrest rates, indicating that there was no additional treatment effect.

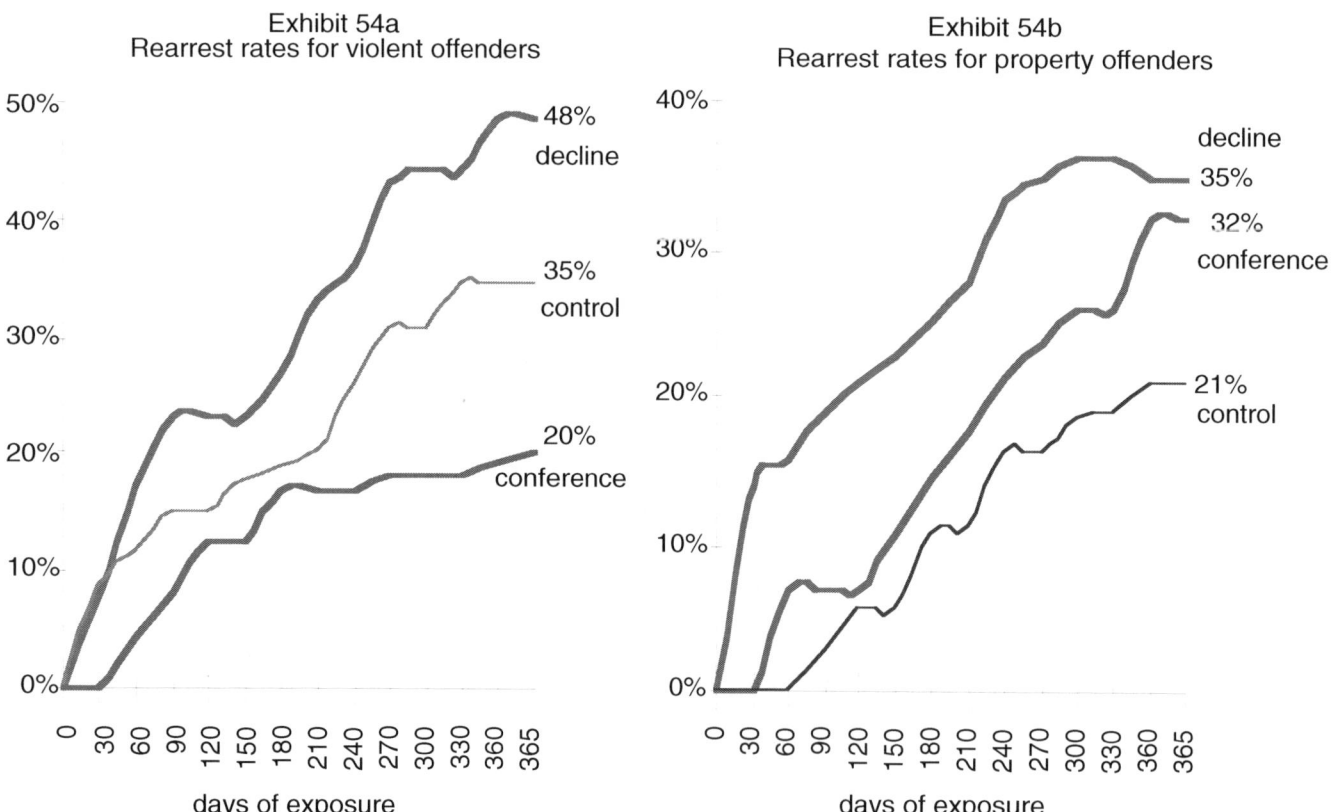

Exhibit 54a
Rearrest rates for violent offenders

Exhibit 54b
Rearrest rates for property offenders

The graph of recidivism rates for the property offenders demonstrates a very different trend than that seen among violent offenders, as shown in Exhibit 54b. Any self-selection bias between conference and decline group property offenders appears to be transitory. Except for differences between the decline group and conference group at 30, 90, 120 and 150 days, differences in the overall trends are not statistically significant. It is curious why control group property offenders appear to have recidivated at such a low rate (see Ch. 7 for further analysis). Other than this low rate for the control group, the results support the hypothesis of a self-selection effect, but no treatment effect (hypothesis #2), among property offenders. However, any self-selection or recidivism suppression effects appear to be transitory, and nonexistent after 12 months of follow-up.

The self-selection hypothesis is further supported when comparing recidivism rates by reasons for declining among offenders in the decline group only. As shown in Exhibit 55, for violent crimes, offenders who declined to participate had a 42 percent rearrest rate, compared to 22 percent for cases where the offender had agreed to participate but the victim declined. Likewise, the difference between the recidivism rates for property offenders is consistent with a self-selection effect that wears off by 12 months, although the number of cases is too small for definitive conclusions.

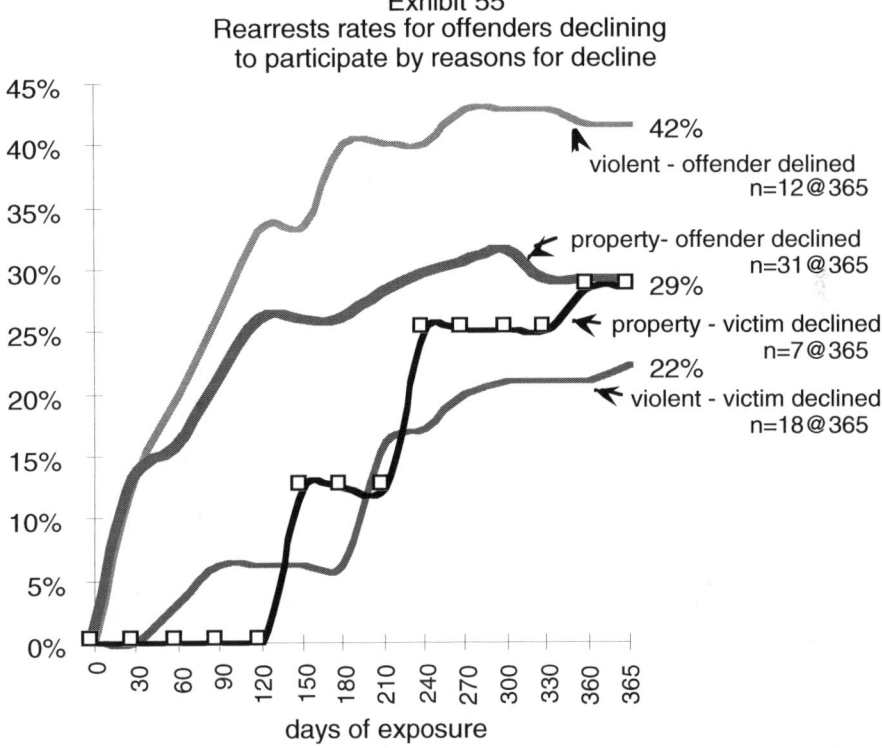

Conclusions

In a preliminary report on the RISE project in Canberra, Australia, the researchers advised that the "evaluation is still at least two years away from learning the answer to the crime prevention question". However, they emphasized that the results "show that conferences work better than court in helping victims to heal" and that "even if we later find that conferences are no more effective than courts in preventing future offending, they might be justified as a better way to help crime victims recover from the crime". (Sherman and Strang, 1997a). This appears to be the case with the Bethlehem conferencing project.

Recidivism rates could have been calculated in a number of ways. Because of the small number of cases in this study, exposure time began following the initial arrest, not following either court or conference "treatments." Measuring recidivism in this way is actually a test of the system's response to reduce reoffending. The difficulty with this kind of field experiment is that other effects cannot be controlled. The young offenders who attended a family group conference may have received sanctions from their parents, some punitive effects from being arrested, and even self-incrimination from being caught. Youths who declined to participate in a conference and youths assigned to the control group both received similar criminal justice interventions. Presumably, any consequences imposed by schools and parents were imposed equally on offenders in the control, conference, and decline groups.

The programmatic effect of conferencing on recidivism for property offenders appears negligible. Without much higher participation rates, positive programmatic effects cannot be demonstrated. However, diverting such cases from formal adjudication processes is beneficial for the justice system by reducing workloads and removing cases that do not appear to need more intensive interventions. The capacity of this process to divert young offenders without increasing reoffense rates makes it a viable court diversion program for moderately serious juvenile offenders.

Conferencing had a significantly different effect on violent cases than on property cases. In spite of the lower participation rates of violent cases, the difference in recidivism persisted beyond the 12-month follow-up period. This result supports the hypothesis that conferencing affects recidivism by resolving conflict between disputing parties rather than any reduction in recidivism from an offender rehabilitation effect. A short-term reduction in recidivism among property offenses suggests that conferencing has a transitory effect consistent with specific deterrent from holding offenders accountable. Confirmation of these operational hypotheses must await future research. The two clear important implication of these results for future research is that crime type matters and must be taken into account, and there is a strong self-selection bias that is related to recidivism rates.

7
Systemic Responses

The present research was designed to maintain the external validity of the experiment; therefore, cases selected for the study should be representative of similar cases not selected and comparable to juvenile arrest cases in other jurisdictions. Thus, if we are to generalize the results for juveniles arrested in Bethlehem to juveniles arrested in other U.S. jurisdictions, we need to consider some specific characteristics of the juveniles arrested in Bethlehem. Since the section on recidivism concluded that the primary effect of the program was to divert from formal processing those youth most likely to have the lowest rearrest rates, two questions arise in the use of this self-selection diversion process: (1) How representative are the selected cases of other juvenile offenders in Bethlehem? and (2) To what proportion of cases in other jurisdictions might these results apply?

Differing jurisdictions in the U.S. have dramatically different juvenile crime problems. The seriousness of the juvenile crime problem locally will determine what proportion of juveniles arrested might be candidates for a police-based restorative diversion. Large urban police departments may be primarily involved with violent gangs, weapons and drugs problems. Perhaps only a small proportion of their juvenile arrests involve crimes like shoplifting or harassment, which comprise a large proportion of the Bethlehem sample. Yet even in large urban areas, these types of charges comprise a significant proportion of juvenile court dockets for youth early in their criminal careers. Offense- and offender-specific information could be used to estimate the proportion of juvenile cases that could be safely diverted in other jurisdictions.

Generalizing the results of the Bethlehem experiment to other jurisdictions depends upon the representativeness of the selected offenders to the more general population of offense- and offender-specific eligible arrests. If the proportion of cases selected for the study is not a representative sample of the eligible pool, this has serious implications for the generalizability of the results. This chapter tests this assumption in light of the recidivism rates for the entire population of juvenile arrests in Bethlehem. In addition, potential changes in the justice processing system by police and magistrates—which may have been unintentional consequences of the experiment—are considered.

Methods

The Bethlehem experiment began November 1, 1995, and ended April 31, 1997, during which the Bethlehem police diverted 80 young people from the formal court system through a restorative justice conference. There were a total of 1,285 juvenile arrests in the 18-month period, with an average number of 71 arrests per month. This was down slightly from the 77-per-month average during the 12 months prior to the experiment.

There was no apparent change in overall arrest patterns during the experimental period as shown in Exhibit 56. The gradual decline in juvenile arrests throughout the period began before the police began conducting diversionary conferences.

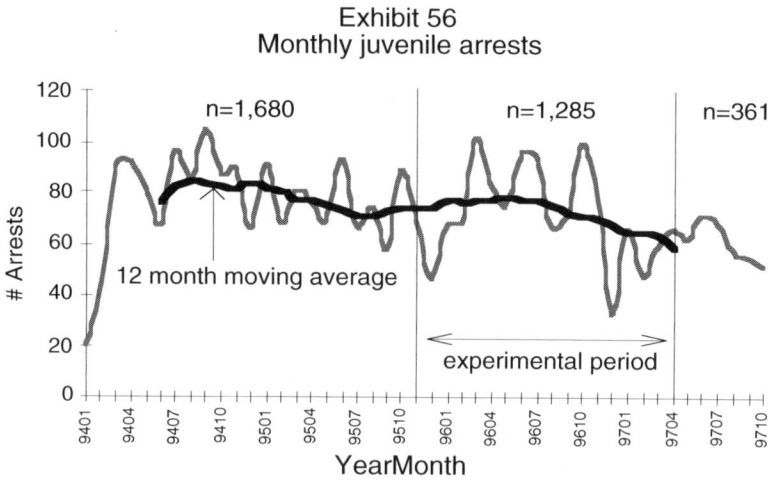

All 3,326 juvenile arrests since 1994 were classified—as best as possible from computerized police arrest data—according to the selection criteria discussed in Chapter 2. The reasons for disqualification were offender history (having a number of prior arrests or a prior adjudication), crime seriousness, inappropriate crime (drug/alcohol offense or no direct victim), case handled informally and non-Bethlehem residents. A series of analyses were conducted among these cases deemed eligible for conferencing to determine the representativeness of the sample used in the study and whether there was any net-widening or other systemic effects from conferencing.

A database of disposition records from the five magistrates serving Bethlehem—including arrests made between January 1, 1993 through September 12, 1997—was also used to fill in any missing dispositions and determine if any changes in magistrate case processing occurred after the experiment began. The database was provided by the Administrative Office of Pennsylvania Courts from a statewide magistrate court database.

Results

As shown in Exhibit 57, 36 percent (1,190) of the arrests were deemed eligible for diversion. The main reason for disqualifying cases related to offender history (28 percent). Interestingly, only 10 percent of arrests were deemed too serious of a crime for diversion, and only 12 percent of arrests were disqualified for solely involving drug or alcohol use or because no direct victim was involved. Those cases that were handled informally (7 percent) and those cases that were ineligible because of out-of-town residency (7 percent) were the smallest group of ineligibles.

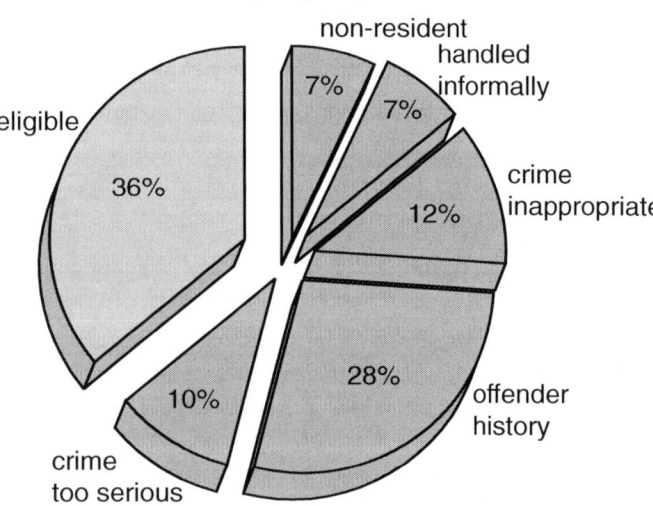

Thus, from the computer eligibility criteria, just over a third of all juvenile arrests could have qualified for the study since the beginning of 1994. However, before we can generalize results to the entire eligible population of arrests, we must consider in what ways the cases selected differ from the non-selected eligibles. If these non-selected cases are similar to selected cases, then the number of possible diversion cases is nearly twice the size suggested by the proportion in the experiment.

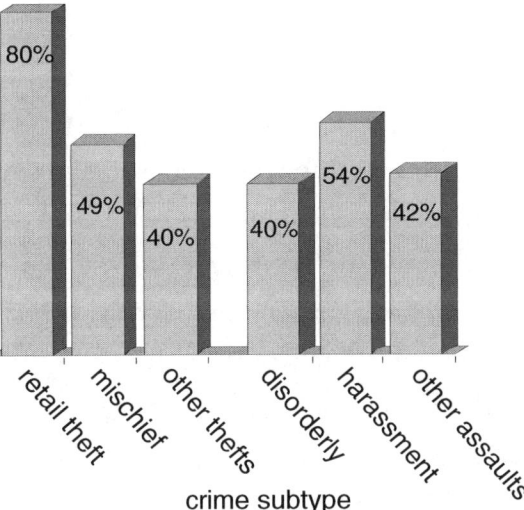

Exhibit 58
Proportion of eligible cases selected during experimental period

Comparing the proportion of eligibles selected during the 18 months of the study does reveal significant differences. Only 56 percent of the 519 cases deemed eligible were actually included in the study. As shown in Exhibit 58, retail theft cases were much more likely than other types of offenses to be selected for the experiment, with 80 percent of eligible retail theft being selected, $\chi^2(5, n = 519) = 64.4$, $p < .001$. Further, while 61 percent of the summary offenses were selected, only 39 percent of misdemeanor offenses were selected, $\chi^2(1, n = 519) = 16.7$, $p < .001$. Also, 64 percent of offenders without any prior arrest were selected, compared to 40 percent of offenders with one to three prior summary arrests, $\chi^2(3, n = 519) = 30.0$, $p < .001$.

There were no significant differences between selected eligibles and non-selected eligibles by the number of current charges or by age, race, gender or zip code. Thus, the computer-generated eligibility criteria is less restrictive than the liaison officer who used arrest report information. Compared to the selected eligibles, those not selected have a somewhat higher crime class, are less likely to have committed retail theft, and are more likely to have prior summary arrests. Otherwise, the non-selected eligibles are statistically similar to the selected eligibles.

When those selected for the study were compared to the non-selected eligibles, controlling for whether the offense was retail theft or not, a specification pattern emerges. Among retail theft cases, 44 percent of the selected offenders were girls compared to 25 percent of non-selected offenders, $\chi^2(1, n = 161) = 3.9$, $p < .05$. Retail theft cases selected were more likely to involve offenders without a prior arrest than non-selected eligible retail thefts, 88 percent versus 41 percent, $\chi^2(3, n = 161) = 39.1$, $p < .001$. These differences were not significant for non-retail theft cases. Thus, the gender differences between the non-selected eligibles and the selected eligibles are only true for retail theft. For non-retail theft cases, the non-selected eligibles are statistically similar to the selected eligibles looking at race, gender, zip code, age, age at first arrest, type of offense, seriousness of current charge and number of prior arrests.

The question remains of whether non-selected eligibles are more at risk than their selected counterparts, perhaps the result of case-specific factors not apparent in the computer data base. When recidivism rates for eligibles not selected are compared with recidivism rates for eligibles selected, an interesting pattern emerges.

Because 80 percent of retail theft eligibles were included in the study, the generalizability of retail theft cases is of less concern than other types of offenses. Presumably, an 80 percent sample of a population will be representative of that population.

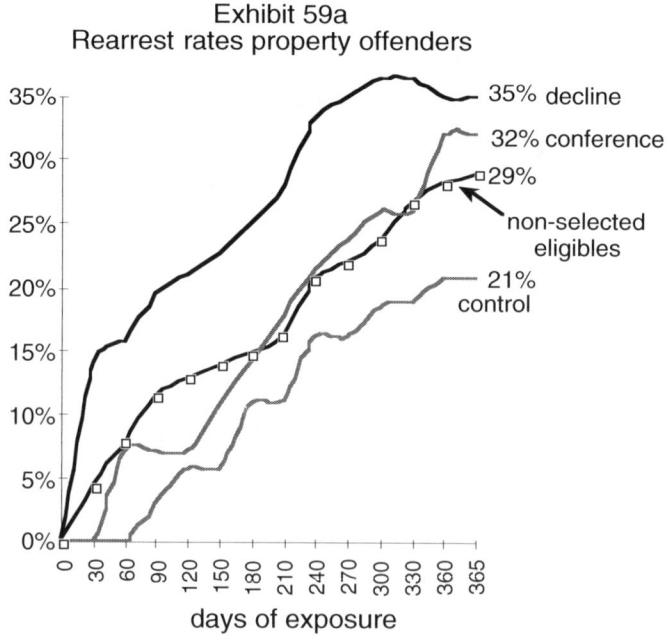

Exhibit 59a
Rearrest rates property offenders

However, the recidivism rate for property offenders in the non-selected eligible group (n=225) looked more like a control group—compared to the conference and decline groups—than the actual control group randomly selected for the experiment as shown in Exhibit 59a. It seems likely then that the randomly selected control group happened (by chance) to include offenders with unusually low recidivism rates, relative to the conference group and the decline group. While this does not change the findings presented in the recidivism section of this study, it does help to explain the unusual control group. It also supports the self-selection hypothesis by suggesting that the short-term, six-month reduction in rearrest rates for property offenders is probably due to the declines being at much higher risk than is generally the case for property offenders.

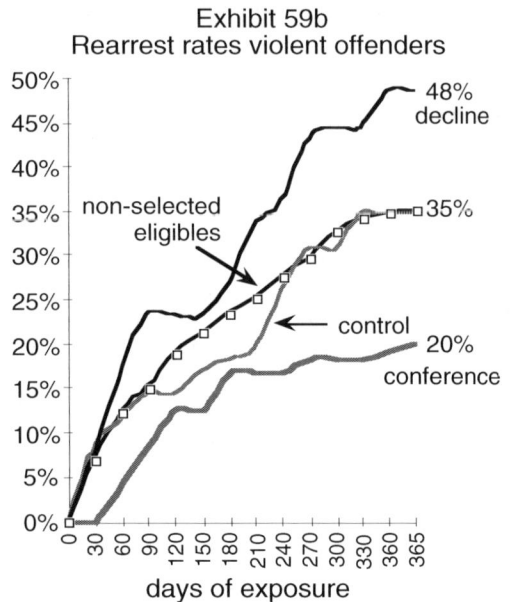

Exhibit 59b
Rearrest rates violent offenders

As can be seen in Exhibit 59b, the violent non-selected eligible group (n=322) is nearly identical to the randomly assigned control group.

Because rearrest data was available for every juvenile offender arrested, it is possible to compare recidivism rates by a number of different factors. When each of the crime subtypes included in the study are compared using the entire arrest population, a clear pattern emerges as seen in Exhibit 60. Those youth charged with one of the violent crimes—harassment, disorderly conduct and assault—have a much higher rearrest rate than those charged with retail theft. In fact, shoplifters generally have the lowest rearrest rate of the crime subtypes (28 percent), and the public order and drug/alcohol offenders not deemed appro-

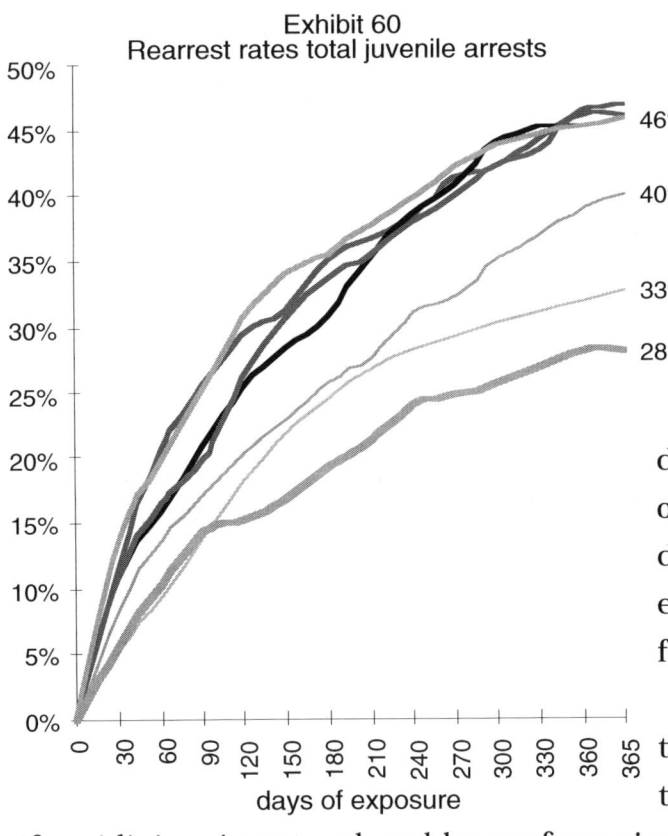

Exhibit 60
Rearrest rates total juvenile arrests

priate for the study had the next lowest rate (33 percent). Criminal mischief was the third lowest recidivism group (40 percent). All categories of violent crimes and personal theft have the highest rearrest rates, virtually indistinguishable from each other at 46 percent. Thus, the absence of an enduring reduction in rearrest rates for property offenders, demonstrated when comparing the decline and conference groups, may be partly explained by the generally low rearrest rate for that offense.

These general recidivism trends suggest that for a police diversionary program, retail theft is a good type of offense to include, even if recidivism is not reduced by conferencing, because of the low reoffense risk for first-time shoplifters. It is, after all, low recidivism offenders who are most appropriately diverted from formal adjudication.

These general recidivism trends also suggest that conferencing is useful for offenders early in their criminal careers before they develop a history of arrests. A rearrest rate of 20 percent for conferenced violent juvenile offenders is especially impressive compared to the 46 percent rates usually seen for these crimes.

The possibility that willingness to participate in a conference is a screen filtering out low-risk youth has additional programmatic implications. As can be seen in Exhibit 61a, property offenders ineligible for the program because they had too extensive of an arrest history clearly were the highest-risk group, with a 12-month rearrest rate of 64 percent. The pool of juvenile offenders who were ineligible because they had committed a felony had a moderately high rearrest rate of 39 percent, though this may be artificially low if the offenders were incarcerated and not at risk of rearrest. Selected cases and non-selected eligibles had moderately low rearrest rates, although many of these are retail theft cases which have the lowest rearrest rate.

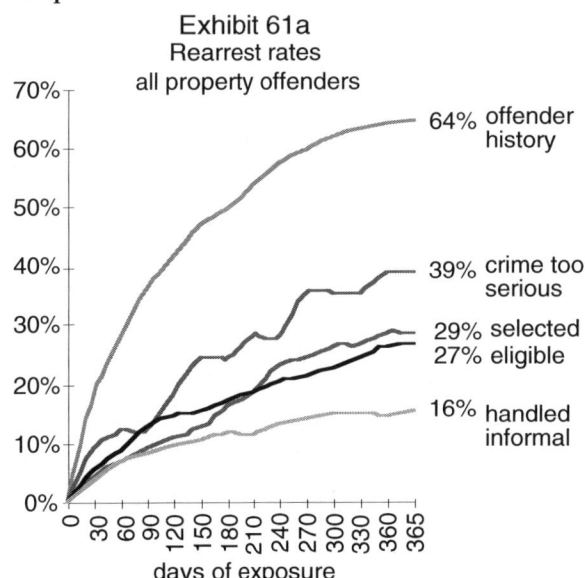

Exhibit 61a
Rearrest rates all property offenders

Juveniles who were handled informally by the police or magistrates were the lowest-risk offenders with a 16 percent rearrest rate. Thus, the offenders included in the study are representative of offenders usually deemed too serious to be informally screened out of the system.

The same pattern of recidivism is evident for violent offenders as shown in Exhibit 61b. Offenders with prior arrest histories are rearrested at a much higher rate (65 percent) than every other violent offender group. However, those violent offenders whose crimes were too serious for police diversion had rearrest rates (32 percent) very similar to those included in the study (37 percent) and their non-selected eligible counterparts (35 percent). Again, those cases handled informally had the lowest rate (24 percent). Except for those with prior histories, all the categories of violent offenders had about 5 percent higher rearrest rates than the corresponding categories for property offenders.

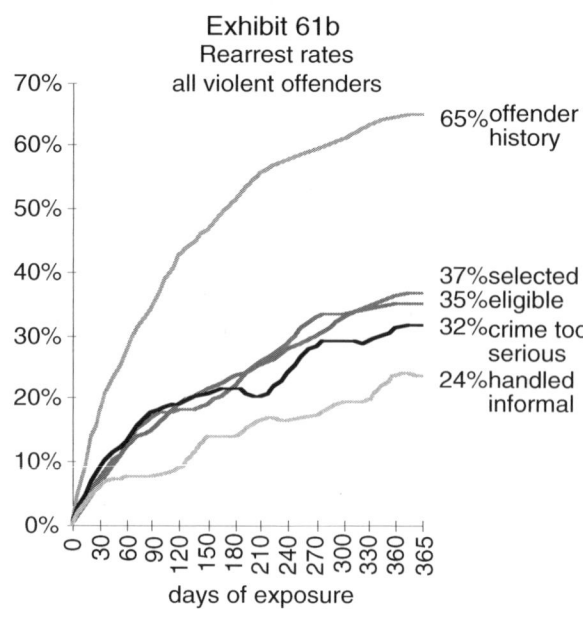

To test the possibility that the police disposed of cases in a different manner during the experiment than they did before (i.e., net-widening), a pre-post comparison of cases by eligibility category should detect a change in arrest disposition. Exhibit 62 shows that the only arrest group to experience a significant decline during the experimental period was the eligible (but not selected) group. Thus, it is evident that most of the cases included in the program were actually diverted from court and did not include youth who would normally have been handled informally.

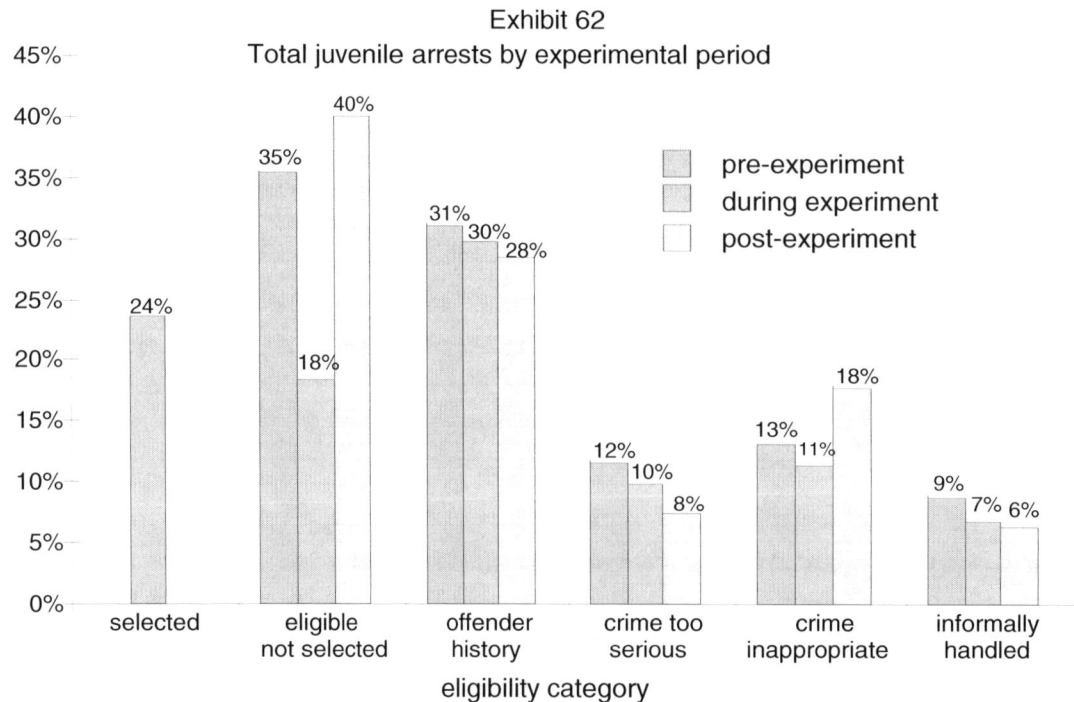

When analyzed as a time series, the number of juvenile arrests per month of non-selected eligibles declines during the experimental period as shown in Exhibit 63. It appears that a majority of eligibles were being selected for the study during the early part of the experiment, and a minority of such cases were selected during the latter period of the experiment. Thus, the selection criteria seem to have become more stringent during the course of the experiment.

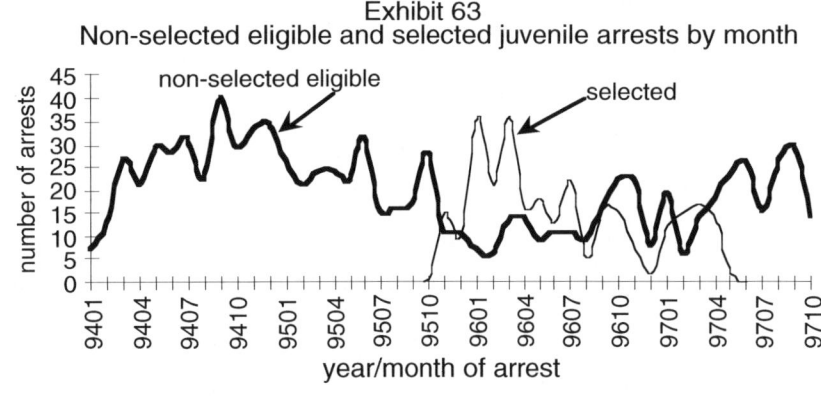

Further, there were not enough cases handled informally to have accounted for the selected offenders. There was an insufficient number of cases handled informally to have produced a net-widening effect, and this is the pool of offenders who would have been affected by net-widening. The time series for the cases disposed of informally shows no disruption from the pattern prior to the experiment as shown in Exhibit 64.

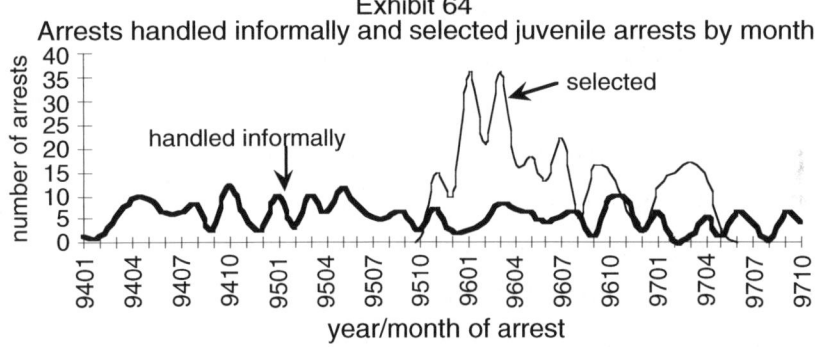

The evidence supports the contention that the only change in police processing of juvenile offenders as a result of the implementation of conferencing was to divert youth who otherwise would have been formally processed. As shown in Exhibit 65, police disposed of 18 percent of cases with known dispositions during the experimental period compared with less than 1 percent prior to implementing conferencing. The decline in the cases disposed by the magistrates demonstrates the court diversion effect of the program. Thus, the project achieved true diversion with no net-widening.

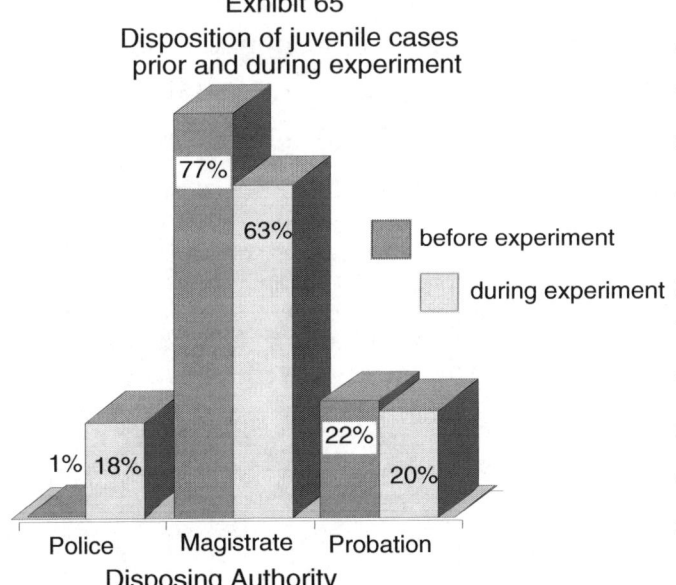

To determine if there were any changes in the manner with which cases were disposed by magistrates, disposition of offenders that were not in the study, but which would have qualified based on offense level and type, were examined (where magistrate disposition information was available). Before the study, 18 per-

Exhibit 66
Disposition of cases not in study
prior to and during study

	total		violent		property	
	prior	during	prior	during	prior	during
n of cases	551	441	276	250	275	191
dropped	18%	18%	21%	20%	14%	16%
acquit	8%	9%	13%	13%	3%	3%
plea	64%	61%	50%	52%	78%	74%
trial	10%	12%	16%	15%	5%	8%

cent of offenders had charges dropped, 6 percent were acquitted, 64 percent made a guilty plea, and 10 percent were found guilty by trial. After the study began, 18 percent of offenders had charges dropped, 9 percent were acquitted, 61 percent made a guilty plea, and 12 percent were found guilty by trial. There were no significant differences between how these cases were disposed before the study began and after the study began by type of offense as shown in Exhibit 66.

Also, the proportions of offenders who were ordered to make a payment of some sort were examined. Before the study, 93 percent of offenders were ordered to make some type of payment. After the study began 90 percent were ordered to make payment. This was not an overall significant difference. Controlling for crime type, however, there was a significant difference among violent offenders, 95 percent pre-study versus 87 percent during the study, $\chi^2(1, n = 347) = 7.3$, $p < .01$. A higher proportion of violent offenders were required to make a payment before the study began than after the study began as shown in Exhibit 67.

Exhibit 67
Percent payment ordered
magistrate cases
prior to and during study

	prior		during	
	%	n	%	n
total	93%	410	90%	322
violent	95%	181	87%	166
property	92%	229	94%	156

The mean payments required were also examined. Before the study, the mean payment was $128.38 ($SD=69.2$, $n=383$). After the study began, the mean payment was $141.46 ($SD=103.4$, $n=290$). This was an overall significant difference. However, controlling for crime type, it was no longer significant for either violent or property offender groups as shown in Exhibit 68.

Exhibit 68
Mean payment ordered — magistrate cases
prior to and during study

	prior to study			during study		
	mean	sd	n	mean	sd	n
total	$128.38	69.16	383	$141.46	103.35	290
violent	$132.52	60.80	172	$143.69	123.56	144
property	$125.00	75.26	211	$139.26	78.90	146

Dispositions of decline and control group cases handled by magistrates were compared to dispositions of cases not in the study but with similar offenses. For offenders not in the study, 16 percent had charges dropped, 8 percent were acquitted, 66 percent made a guilty plea, and 11 percent were found guilty by trial. For cases in the study, 20 percent had charges dropped, 9 percent were acquitted, 63 percent made a guilty plea, and 8 percent were found guilty by trial. These were not significant differences. However, controlling for crime type, there was a significant difference among property offenders, $\chi^2(3, n = 829) = 11.3$, $p < .05$. Cases in the study had higher proportions of dropped charges and acquittals, and lower proportions of guilty pleas and guilt by trial, than

Exhibit 69
Dispositions comparison

	total		violent		property	
	not in study	in study	not in study	in study	not in study	in study
n of cases	1658	141	913	57	745	84
dropped	16%	20%	18%	21%	13%	19%
acquit	8%	9%	12%	11%	3%	8%
plea	66%	63%	56%	53%	78%	70%
trial	11%	8%	14%	16%	6%	2%

cases not in the study as shown in Exhibit 69.

The proportion of offenders not in the study where payment was ordered was 86 percent. For those in the study, it was 83 percent. There were no significant differences in proportion of offenders required to make payments between study and non-study groups as shown in Exhibit 70.

Exhibit 70
Percent payment ordered magistrate cases prior to and during study

	not in study %	n	in study %	n
total	86%	1270	83%	100
violent	84%	644	85%	39
property	87%	626	82%	61

Mean payments for offenders not in the study were $139.52 ($SD = 91.2$, $n = 1086$), compared to $120.88 for offenders in the study ($SD = 52.63$, $n = 83$). There were no significant differences in the mean payment required between study and non-study groups as shown in Exhibit 71.

Exhibit 71
Mean payment ordered — magistrate cases prior to and during study

	prior to study			during study		
	mean	stdev	n	mean	stdev	n
total	$128.38	69.16	383	$141.46	103.35	290
violent	$132.52	60.80	172	$143.69	123.56	144
property	$125.00	75.26	211	$139.26	78.90	146

Conclusions

Among retail theft cases, non-selected eligibles had a somewhat higher crime class and were more likely to have prior summary arrests than selected cases. Otherwise, the non-selected eligibles were statistically similar to the selected cases.

For retail theft cases, it appears that the randomly selected control group happened (by chance) to include offenders with unusually low recidivism rates, relative to the conference group and the decline group.

The project achieved true diversion without net-widening effects. The general recidivism trends suggest that retail theft is a good type of offense to include in a diversionary program, even if recidivism is not reduced, because of the low reoffense risk for first-time shoplifters. Also, it seems evident that the voluntary nature of the program creates a selecting process that diverts those offenders least likely to reoffend.

There did not appear to be any substantial differences in the manner in which magistrates disposed of cases before the study began versus after the study began. A higher proportion of violent offenders were required to make a payment before the study began than after the study began, which is opposite of what would have been expected by the removal of lesser serious violent offenders from formal processing. This suggests the violent offenders participating in the conferences would likely have paid court fines without the diversion.

During the experimental period, cases in the study disposed by the magistrate courts had higher proportions of dropped charges and acquittals, and lower proportions of guilty pleas and guilt by trial, than cases not in the study. This suggests that cases selected for the study were cases likely to have plead guilty. The proportion of remaining cases dismissed by the court would have increased because some of the guilty pleas were diverted from the denominator.

8
Comparative Analyses

Despite the very different philosophies guiding formal adjudication processes versus restorative justice processes, it is worth pursuing ways in which conferences compare to formal adjudication processes. Braithwaite urges a systemic solution to the problem of breaching certain upper limits for sanctions:

> Conferences should be constrained not only against any incarcerative order but also against any order which is more punitive in its effects than courts typically impose for such offenses. In other words, offenders should be able to appeal to juvenile courts to have overturned any intervention which is more severe than a court would have imposed. An advocacy group . . . should be given state resources to monitor outcomes of conferences . . . looking for cases for which it should be suggested to the defendant that s/he might do better to have the case reheard before a court. Under such a system, conferencing would result in fewer breaches of upper limits than juvenile court adjudication of the same types of cases. (Braithwaite, 1994, p.204)

The other side of this is the concern that outcomes from conferences may be too lenient, below some lower limit of proportionality. Through a retributive lens, this is certainly a concern. Through a restorative lens, it is only a concern insofar as the intervention is insufficient in preventing negative consequences. Braithwaite comments:

> It is true that breaches of lower proportionality limits would be increased by conferencing. Often victims prefer to forgive and forget, or even to offer to give the young offender some help rather than demand any punishment . . . I do not believe there is any such thing as a disproportionately low sanction, as a matter of justice versus mercy. (Braithwaite, 1994, pp.204-5)

In order to put into perspective the outcomes of police-based restorative conferencing for juveniles, it is necessary to compare these results with other disposition possibilities for such cases. First we will compare the conference outcomes with the outcomes for the cases in the study who were referred to court (the control and decline groups). Since restorative justice processes are very different than court, it is also instructive to compare the results from this study with results reported on other restorative justice programs, primarily victim-offender mediation.

Methods

All cases in the study were tracked to determine the eventual case outcome for cases disposed prior to October 1, 1997. Conference data was obtained through conference observations and interviews with the program liaison officer. Disposition data for control and decline group cases was obtained through the Bethlehem Police database and a statewide magistrate database mentioned in Chapter 7. Victim and offender satisfaction and perceptions of fairness data was obtained through participant surveys. The present Bethlehem study used many of the survey instruments from Umbreit's mediation studies (1994). Additional information on victim-offender mediation programs was obtained from published results of four studies: Umbreit (1994) compared victim-offender mediation (VOM) programs in Albuquerque, N.M., Minneapolis, Minn., Oakland, Ca., and Austin, Tx.; Umbreit and Roberts (1996) compared VOM programs in Coventry and Leeds, U.K.; Umbreit (1996) compared VOM programs in four Canadian provinces; and Coates (1985) and Coates (1985) and Coates and Gehm (1989) compared early VOM programs in one county in Ohio and four counties in Indiana (the 1989 study included three additional counties).

Family group conferencing is one of the latest developments in restorative justice practices (McCold, 1997). Previously, most research in restorative justice has been limited to victim-offender mediation (VOM), the bulk of which has been done by Mark Umbreit and associates.

There are a number of differences between conferences and mediation. Mediation limits participation to victims and offenders and excludes family and other supporters from direct participation. Some VOM programs allow parents to observe the mediation, but many VOM programs feel that offenders are less likely to express honest feelings with such parties present. Conferences always include at least one parent of the offender and encourage other family and important social supporters of both victims and offenders to directly participate in the process. But conferencing is not just mediation with more participants (as suggested by Van Ness, 1997).

Mediators are much more likely to feel that they need to develop a personal rapport and trusting relationship between themselves and offenders and victims prior to the mediation (although this was not the case in the Austin VOM discussed below), and stress the importance of the mediator being seen as a neutral party in the dispute. Conferences begin with the assumption that a wrong has been done and the offender has an obligation to repair that wrong as much as possible (hardly a neutral position). Conference facilitators do not attempt to create special relationships of trust between themselves and conference participants, but rely on the bonds of trust which exists between victims and their supporters and offenders and their supporters. Thus, VOM is much more dependent upon the skills and capacities of the mediator to make the process work. Conferences assume that the facilitator is only providing a forum for the affected parties to work through to their own resolution, merely providing a consistent process for such resolution to occur. Thus the success of conferences is much less dependent upon the skills and capacities of the facilitator, and much more trusting of the process and participants.

Both VOM and conferences can be used at various stages of criminal processes. Mediation programs are likely to be operated as adjuncts to court services or prosecution services and may employ specially trained professional mediators or trained and screened community volunteers. Conferencing programs may operate as adjuncts to court services and have also been implemented using trained community volunteers. However, only conferencing encourages criminal justice personnel themselves to facilitate the process, including probation and corrections officers. While the Bethlehem Experiment used trained police officers, conferencing is by no means limited to police-based restorative processes.

Both VOM and conferencing generally assume that participation of victims and offenders must be voluntary and that either party may choose traditional court processes if that is their wish. The voluntary nature of restorative processes may be a limiting factor in some cases, but voluntary participation is central to either model in their pure forms. However, this does create a problem for the scientific evaluation of such programs since participation rates will vary from program to program and strict random assignment of cases is problematic.

While the present study used trained on-duty police officers to set up and conduct conferences, the mediation programs we will compare our results to differ in the sponsorship and management of their programs. The Albuquerque, Minneapolis and Oakland VOM programs are operated by private not-for-profit agencies using volunteer mediators. The Austin victim-offender reconciliation program is operated by both the juvenile probation office and a not-for-profit agency using professional mediators. All of these programs are for moderately serious juvenile offenders. Together, 87 percent of their cases were property offenses, and of the cases handled, 69 percent were pre-adjudicatory diversion (Umbreit, 1994, pp.43-59).

The four Canadian VOM programs in Langley, Calgary, Winnipeg and Ottawa are run by not-for-profit organizations. Types of offenses addressed were primarily assaults, followed by property offenses, including vandalism, theft and burglary. The sessions were mostly used as pre-trial diversion. The Winnipeg and Ottawa sites addressed mostly adult crimes, while the Langley and Calgary sites addressed mostly juvenile crimes. Volunteer mediators as well as trained professionals conducted the mediation sessions (Umbreit and Roberts, 1996).

The Coventry and Leeds programs were run by probation service agencies. They dealt primarily with assault, burglary and theft cases, committed both by juveniles and adults. Cases were referred by courts following a guilty plea. Mediators were trained professionals. These two programs allowed for indirect mediation, involving shuttle negotiations between victims and offenders without meeting face-to-face and thus had a much lower direct mediation proportion than traditional VOM programs (Umbreit and Roberts, 1996).

Cases mediated in the sites in the five-county U.S. study were mostly court-referred or court-ordered, as pre-trial diversion or as a condition of sentencing. Offenses included burglary, theft, vandalism, fraud and assault. Seventy-three percent of offenders were juveniles. Two-thirds of the mediators were trained community volunteers, the rest professionals.

Clearly, offenders and cases are not necessarily directly comparable between these programs. Some of these programs addressed offenses similar to those in the Bethlehem Experiment. Others addressed some more serious offenses in addition. The Bethlehem Experiment was a police diversionary program, using trained police officers to conduct the meetings, while the other programs were diversionary and conditions of sentencing, using trained professionals and volunteers to conduct the meetings. Despite these differences, comparisons are worthwhile to benchmark relative performance of police conferencing. It will remain for future research to determine whether the differences in programs are due to differing types of cases, differences in program auspices, or the effects of including a wider circle of the community directly in the process.

Results

Conference versus Court

Offenders who participated in family group conferences had to admit responsibility for the offense charged. During the conference process, they were asked to describe what they did, what they were thinking about when they did it, and how people were affected. They then heard from their victims and their family about how others were affected and what they thought about what the offender had done. Then, all participants were directed by the police officer facilitating the conference to come up with some way to "repair the harm" caused by the offender's actions. During this time, offenders often apologized for what they did, sometimes prompted by others, sometimes by their own volition. Once participants came to agreement on reparative action needed in the case, the conference was ended and there was an informal period where participants had refreshments and signed the agreement contract. Agreements often included community service. For many retail theft cases, stores insisted that offenders comply with paying a $150 civil demand. In a few cases where damage was incurred, offenders agreed to restitution payments. Often there were agreements for written or personal apologies to people not present at the conference, and other reparative or problem-solving actions.

Offenders who went through formal adjudication had to enter a plea to the magistrate and then attend a hearing, probably accompanied by a parent. If they pled guilty, they may have been assigned to an accelerated disposition program or required to pay fines, costs, and/or restitution. If they pled not guilty, the complainant or police officer may have been asked to present evidence, which would have been reviewed by the magistrate. If a complainant did not show, or the magistrate deemed the evidence insufficient, charges may have been dismissed or withdrawn. If they were found guilty, offenders may have been required to pay fines, costs and/or restitution. The magistrate may have lectured to them about their inappropriate behavior and tried to discover why the offender committed the crime. They also may have assigned some community service if the offender was not able to easily pay the fine, or required the offender to write an essay about what they did and why they shouldn't have done it. Some magistrates require offenders to tour a local prison or attend classes about shoplifting.

Exhibit 72
Disposition of court-assigned cases in study

	total	decline	control	property	violent
n of cases	141	60	81	84	57
dropped charge	20%	20%	20%	19%	21%
acquitted	9%	13%	6%	8%	11%
guilty plea	63%	60%	65%	70%	53%
guilty by trial	8%	7%	9%	2%	16%

Analysis was conducted of dispositions and average outcomes of cases in the study that went through formal adjudication. As shown in Exhibit 72, 20 percent of offenders had charges dropped, 9 percent were acquitted, 63 percent made a guilty plea, and 8 percent were found guilty by trial. Among the decline group offenders with disposition information, 46 percent pled guilty ($n = 28$). Property offenders were more likely to make a guilty plea than violent offenders. However, controlling for experimental group, this difference was only significant among offenders in the control group, $\chi^2(3, n = 81) = 5.74$, $p < .01$. Thus, property offenders in the control group were different from offenders in other groups in that they were more likely to make a guilty plea, even when controlling for reason for decline, as shown in Exhibit 73, $\chi^2(4, n = 161) = 12.8$, $p < .05$.

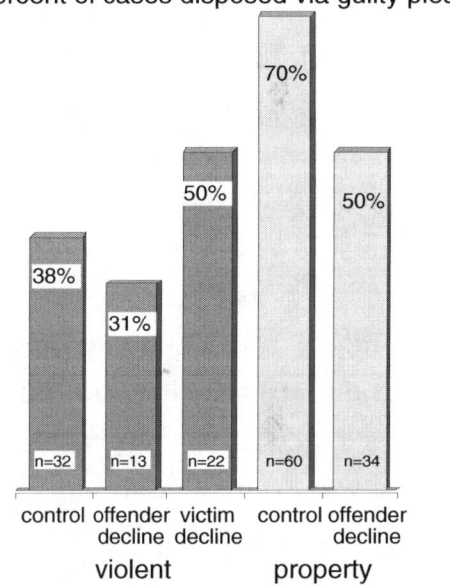

Exhibit 73
Percent of cases disposed via guilty plea

The average time from offense to disposition was 69 days, ranging from 2 to 426 days. For control group offenders the average time was 89 days ($SD = 90.0$, $n = 91$), and for decline group offenders the average time was 49 days ($SD = 55.3$, $n = 97$), which was a statistically significant difference, $F(1, 186) = 13.4$, $p < .001$.

Among cases where offenders made a guilty plea, the average time from offense to disposition was 35 days for the control group ($SD = 39.1$, $n = 54$) and 57 days for the decline group ($SD = 83.0$, $n = 34$). For conferenced cases, time from offense to conference was 37 days ($SD = 25.8$, $n = 80$). Differences between the three experimental groups were not statistically significant. Courts disposed 60 percent of cases within a month where offenders made a guilty plea ($n = 88$), compared to only 45 percent of conferenced cases ($n = 80$), $\chi^2(1, n = 168) = 3.9$, $p < .05$. Therefore, where offenders made a guilty plea, court was more efficient than the conferencing program in disposing of cases within a month.

Of those offenders who were found guilty (plea or trial), 83 percent had to make a payment of some variety—fines, costs or restitution. There were no differences between control and decline groups, or property and violent offender groups in the proportion ordered to make such payments.

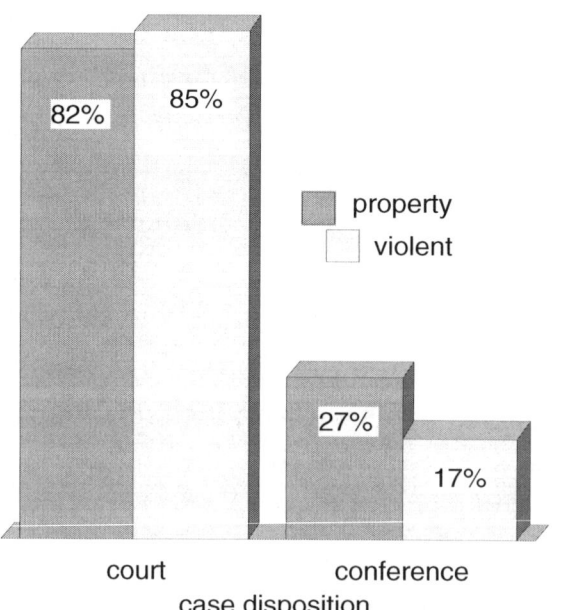

Exhibit 74
Proportion of guilty offenders paying monetary costs

Since all offenders participating in a conference are required to admit they committed the acts charged, presumably they would have all pled guilty had their cases been disposed by formal court processes. Thus, comparing the proportions of types of dispositions between court and conference cases is problematic. However, it is possible to compare the sentences for those who are found guilty by a plea or trial with those whose cases disposed by a conference. As shown in Exhibit 74, the proportion required to make payments was much higher among the court cases in the study than among the conference cases, χ^2 (1, n = 180) = 63.5, $p < .001$.

Where payments were required of offenders by court, they averaged $120.88, ranging from $31 to $362.50 ($SD$ = 52.63, n = 83). Among property offenders, the mean payment was $114.53 ($SD$ = 60.02, n = 50). Among violent offenders, the mean payment was $130.49 ($SD$ = 37.72, n = 33). This was not a significant difference. The mean payment for offenders in the decline group was $135.25 ($SD$ = 64.19, n = 33). The mean payment for offenders in the control group was $111.39 ($SD$ = 41.39, n = 50). Decline group offenders were levied higher average payments than control group offenders. However, when crime type was controlled for, differences in costs between control and decline groups was only significant among property offenders, $F(1, 48) = 5.93$, $p < .05$. Thus, property offenders in the decline group were levied higher payments than property offenders in the control group.

Because of the routine demand for civil judgments from two of the large retail stores participating in the study, costs for property offenders conferenced was higher than costs for violent offenders conferenced. Presumably, these same civil demands were placed on offenders shoplifting from these two stores whose cases were disposed in court, but the $150 is in addition to the fines and costs imposed by court making difference in the cost associated with property offender cases disposed in court greater than that shown in Exhibit 75. Thus, the amount of costs for the small proportion of cases conferenced who agreed to pay restitution or civil demands was much lower than the amount ordered by the magistrates.

One difference between conference and court outcomes were that conferenced offenders were much more likely to have been assigned community service and other types of reparative actions and court-processed offenders were more likely to have been required to make a payment. Part of the difficulty in making such comparisons between court and conference outcomes is that the magistrate's court is limited in their capacity to order community service. Many times when an offender does receive community service from the court, it is in exchange for an accelerated disposition of their case and the charges are withdrawn upon completion of their community service hours. Information on such court-ordered outcomes was unavailable from computerized court records.

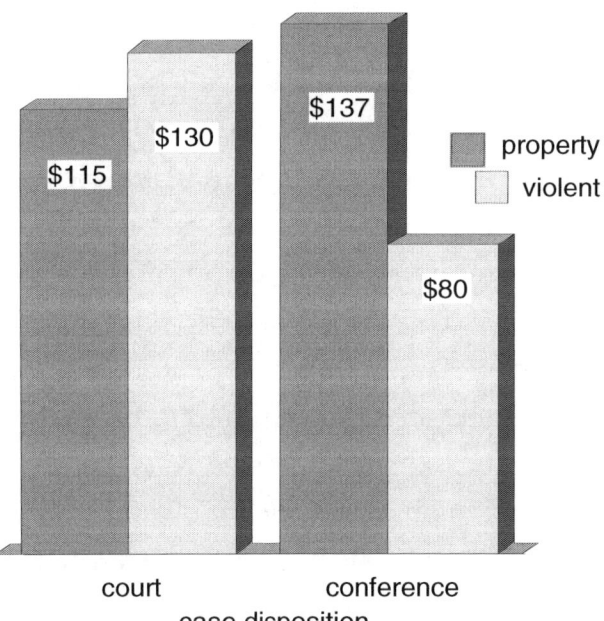

Exhibit 75
Mean monetary costs for offenders paying costs

Since retail theft cases were routinely asked to perform 40 hours of community service by two of the larger retailers participating in the conferences, there is the general sense that, at least for property cases, offenders were agreeing to harsher outcomes than they would have received in court. This is certainly the case for a 13-year-old girl who completed 40 hours of community service for the theft of one candy bar. However, since many of the violent crime victims were satisfied with only a sincere apology in conferences, violent offenders were treated more harshly in court than they were in conferences.

Conference versus Mediation

Participation rates were measured as the proportion of cases participating among the cases referred to the program. As shown in Exhibit 76, the participation rate for the Bethlehem Experiment (42 percent) was higher than those rates reported for the VOM programs (28 to 40 percent). The two British VOM programs allow victims and offenders to participate indirectly through shuttle negotiations without meeting face-

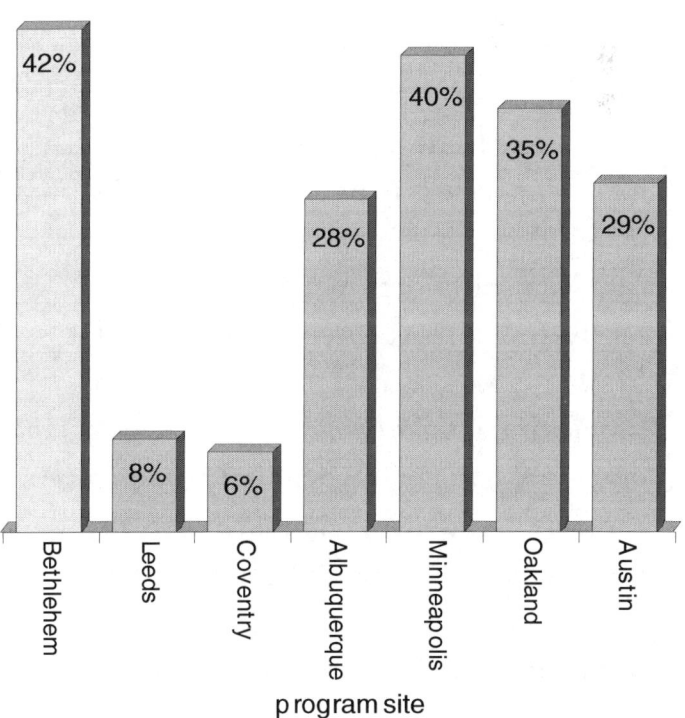

Exhibit 76
Participation rates

to-face and thus had a much lower direct mediation proportion than traditional VOM programs (Umbreit and Roberts, 1996). The relatively high participation rate for a police-based conferencing program is something of a surprise, and concerns raised by VOM advocates that victims and offenders are less trusting of police than they would be of an impartial community volunteer seem unfounded. The fact that the majority of cases referred to mediation or conferencing opt for traditional court process demonstrates that participation is truly voluntary.

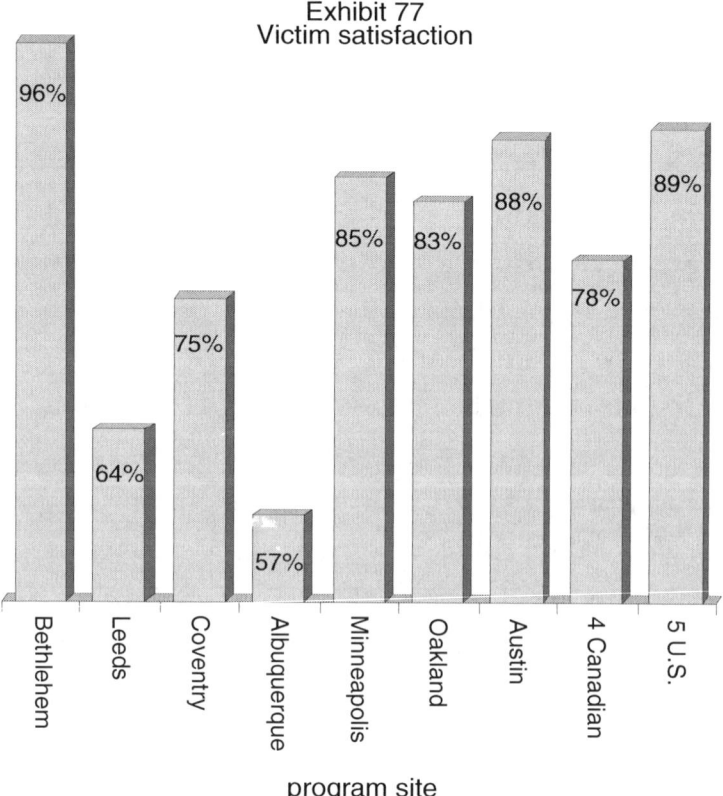

Restorative justice is a more balanced approach to crime and considers victim participation and healing as a significant goal of the process. Thus, victim satisfaction is a critical dimension in evaluating the success of these programs. As shown in Exhibit 77, the conferences conducted by the Bethlehem Police produced higher victim satisfaction than all the VOM programs, much higher than the Albuquerque and British programs. Among victims of violent crimes, conferencing received a 100 percent victim satisfaction rating.

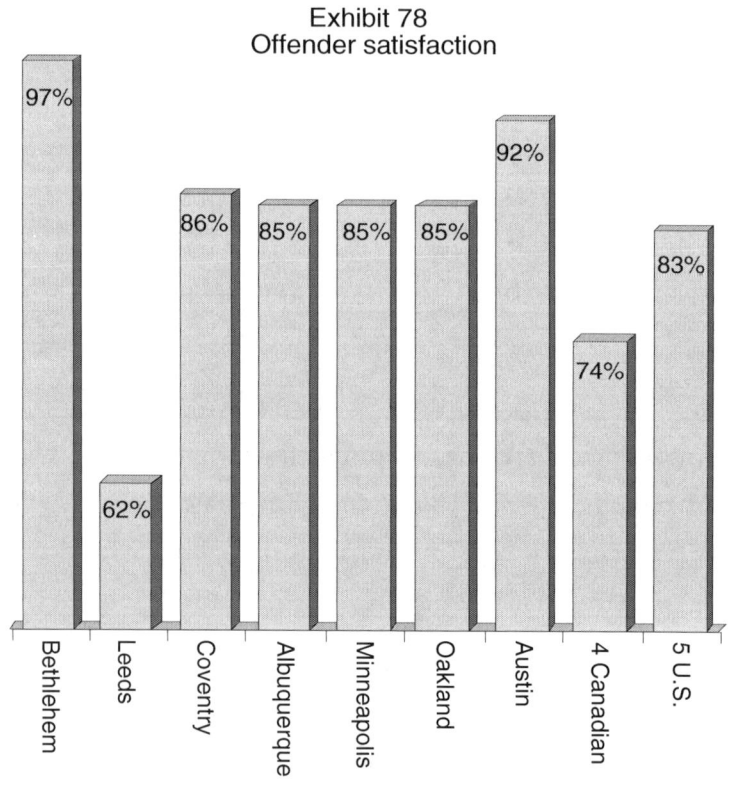

Since one purpose of restorative justice practices is to help the offender learn from their behavior, it is important that offenders participate voluntarily and are treated with respect. Thus, offender satisfaction is also an important measure of successful programs. As shown in Exhibit 78, 97 percent of offenders participating in the present study expressed general satisfaction with the way their case was handled. This is also higher than that reported from the mediation studies, and much higher than the Leeds program and the four Canadian VOM programs. Only the professionally run program in Austin had offender satisfaction ratings comparable to ratings from police-based conferences in the present study.

It is possible that while victims and offenders felt that their case was handled in a manner that satisfied them, they may have felt that something about the process was unfair to them. As shown in Exhibit 79, 96 percent of victims in the present study rated conferencing as fair, higher than any of the mediation programs evaluated (67 to 89 percent).

Likewise, offenders rated the police-based conferencing process as fair in 97 percent of the cases. Offenders in the Minneapolis, Oakland and Austin VOM programs also rated the process as fair in more than 90 percent of the cases (90 to 94 percent), and the VOM program at Coventry received the lowest offender satisfaction rating (71 percent) as shown in Exhibit 80.

Victims in both types of restorative programs had high overall satisfaction ratings and perceptions of fairness with the way the case was handled. Victims' perception of fairness of the agreement to themselves was 96 percent in the present study and 89 percent in Umbreit's multi-site VOM study. Victim perception of fairness of the agreement to the offender was 98 percent in the present study and 92 percent in the VOM study.

Offenders also rated these variables high in both types of restorative

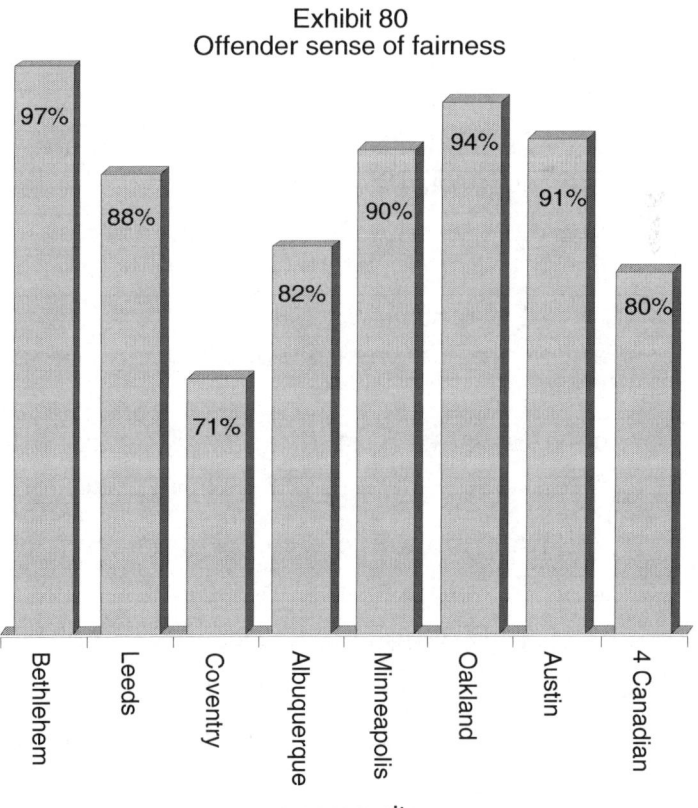

Exhibit 79
Victim sense of fairness

Exhibit 80
Offender sense of fairness

programs. Offender satisfaction was 97 percent in the present study and 87 percent in the multi-site VOM study. Perception of fairness with the way the case was handled was 97 percent in the present study and 89 percent in the VOM study. Offender perception of fairness of the agreement to the victim was 96 percent in the present study and 93 percent in the VOM study. Offender perception of fairness of the agreement to the offender was 93 percent in the present study and 88 percent in the VOM study.

In the Bethlehem Experiment, 94 percent of offenders complied with the agreements reached, which replicates Moore's (1995) original Wagga findings. In the multi-site VOM study, the rates of restitution completion were 77 percent in Minneapolis and 93 percent in Albuquerque. The five-county U.S. study had a completion rate of 90 percent for performing service for victims; the authors reported that more than 80 percent of financial restitution contracts had been completed at the time of their review of records (Coates and Gehm, 1989). The studies in Canada and the U.K. cited above did not report on agreement compliance.

Braithwaite (1997) reports on studies citing restitution completion rates, including:

- A review of restorative justice programs in the U.S., Canada and Great Britain revealing reparation and compensation completion rates between 64 and 100 percent (Haley and Neugebauer, 1992)
- A study of mediation programs in Britain, showing an 80 percent rate of agreement completion (Marshall, 1992)
- A study of mediation programs in New Zealand with 58 percent completion of agreements (Galaway, 1992)
- A Finnish study reporting 85 percent completion of agreements reached through mediation (Iivari, 1992)
- A study of a mediation program in England, with 91 percent of agreements honored in full (Dignan, 1992)
- A study of three pilot victim-offender reconciliation projects in West Germany with a 76 percent full completion rate (Trenczek, 1990)
- A study of Canadian victim-offender reconciliation programs with agreement compliance rates between 90 and 95 percent in Alberta and 99 percent in Calgary (Pate, 1990)
- A report on South Australian conferences finding 86 percent full compliance with conference agreements (Wundersitz and Hetzel, 1996)

Satisfaction and a general experience of fairness were significantly higher in the FGC study for both victims and offenders than for the multi-site VOM study, as shown in Exhibit 81 and Exhibit 82. Differences in perceptions of fairness of the restitution agreement to victim and offender were not significant. Thus police-based conferences produced greater victim satisfaction, greater offender satisfaction, greater victim sense of fairness and greater offender sense of fairness than the VOM studies considered. Police-based conferences produced at least as high victim and offender sense of fairness with outcomes

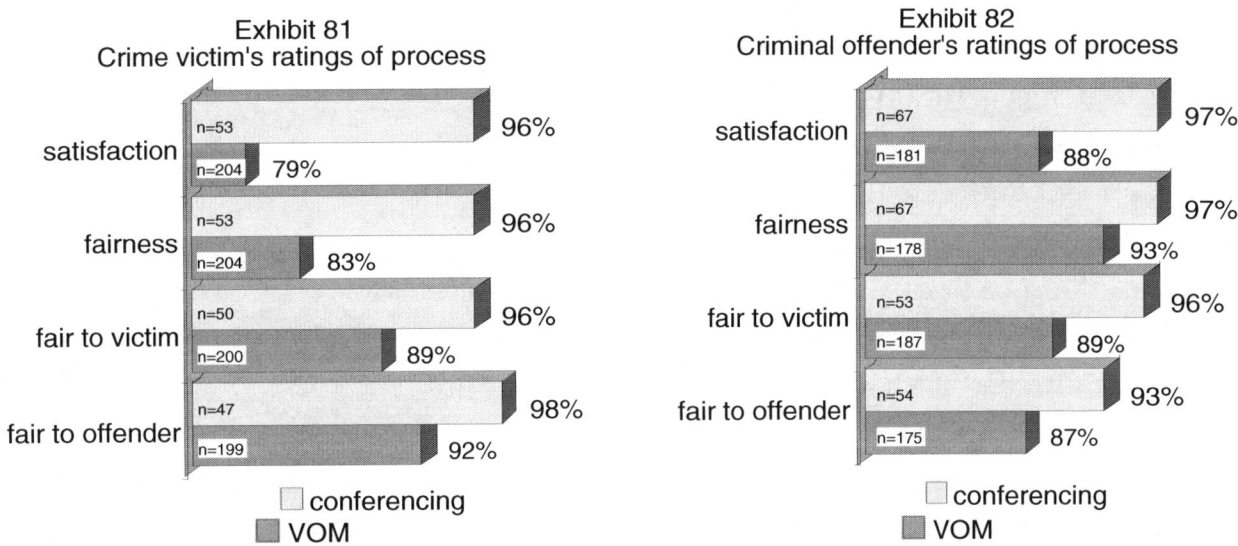

Exhibit 81
Crime victim's ratings of process

Exhibit 82
Criminal offender's ratings of process

as the multi-site VOM study. The agreement compliance rates in the Bethlehem study are comparable to those cited in other mediation and conferencing studies.

Perhaps one of the most important distinctions between police-based conferencing and VOM is the cost of program operation. Each of the four sites in Umbreit's multi-site VOM study operate as stand-alone mediation projects with staff, budgets and volunteer recruitment and training plans. The costs per unit of mediation for each of these mediation projects can be calculated by dividing the program budget for a year by the number of cases mediated per year to produce a unit cost of mediation. Such straightforward computations of the cost for police-based conferencing is not possible. There is no separate program operation budget for this type of conferencing. Police officers are expected to set up and conduct conferences as part of their regular duties, thus requiring no additional operational expenses for the department. However, for rough comparisons, approximations of the number of officer hours away from other police duties can be used to estimate the trade-off costs to the department.

The average conference lasted 33 minutes with 5 minutes of social time afterward. The facilitating officers spent less than an hour to arrange and prepare for the average conference. The project liaison officer used about 30 minutes per case screening out ineligible cases and making initial contact with participants. Arresting officers in addition to the facilitating officers participated in 25 percent of the conferences. Thus, the average number of department man-hours was 2.3 hours per conference. At the current senior patrolman salary of $26.33 per hour, the average salary cost to the department per conference was $59.70.

Additionally, the department would have incurred training costs had the officers not been trained through scholarships. The training tuition cost of $235 for each of the 20 officers trained was $4,700. Three eight-hour shifts for each of the officers trained also cost the department an additional 480 man-hours or $12,638.40. Thus the department (would have) incurred an additional $17,338.40 or $267 per conference training expense. Costs for ongoing supervision and in-service training are not included in this estimate.

While the operation costs for on-duty police officers to conduct restorative conferences may not be visible in the department budget, even if we include the salary costs with the initial training costs to the department, the total cost per conference for the 18-month period of the project is $399 per conference. As shown in Exhibit 83, this is well below the unit cost of all but one of the mediation programs evaluated in Umbreit's multi-site study.

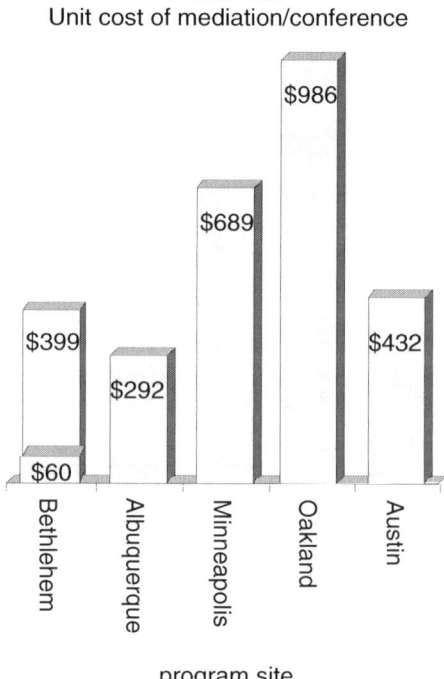

The initial start-up cost for the department creates an ongoing capacity to conduct conferences. Most of this expense was salary costs for the 20 officers to participate in, what was then, the three-day training. Real Justice is now providing two-day trainings which would reduce salary costs for having officers trained by a third. Because of the large number of officers trained in Bethlehem, the $17,338 training costs is probably not a good estimate of the start-up costs for other police departments, who generally train a few officers at a time. Further, the start-up costs for a department is an investment in a capacity that should continue for a good number of years, spreading out this initial cost over more than the 18 months considered in this study, eventually returning total cost per conference to the man-hour only figure of $60.

Conclusions

Police-based restorative conferences produced outcomes for offenders comparable in some respects to the court process. Conferenced juvenile offenders were less likely to be required to pay monetary compensation or fines but were more likely to be required to perform community service hours than similar offenders processed through the traditional court system. Conferences produced outcomes for property offenders that tended to be harsher than would have been imposed by court, and conferences for violent offenders tended to produce outcomes for offenders that might be seen as less harsh than courts might have imposed.

When compared to another current restorative justice programs not operated by police, police-based restorative conferences fare very well. The Bethlehem Police Department's "Operation P.R.O.J.E.C.T" had a higher participation rates, included a larger proportion of violent offenses, and produced higher victim and offender satisfaction and perceptions of fairness than the mediation programs. Further, these police-based conferences were rated by the victims as fair to themselves and their offenders, and outcomes that were rated by the offenders as fair to themselves and their victims as victims and offenders participating in the mediation programs considered. Compliance with conference agreements was 94 percent, replicating the finding in Wagga Wagga and are comparable to agreement compliance rates reported in other mediation and conferencing studies.

Overall program costs for the police-based conferencing program appear to be no greater than costs for the mediation programs, and may be as much as ten times less expensive to operate than the mediation programs considered. Once police officers are trained, they can conduct conferences as part of their on-duty tasks, as part of a general community and problem-oriented policing approach to problems of juvenile crime, with little additional expense to the department beyond the normal duties of their officers.

9
Conclusions

Let us now return to the concerns and questions posed in the introduction and attempt to answer them in light of the research findings. The six questions were:

1. Can typical American police officers conduct conferences consistent with due process and restorative justice principles?
2. Does conferencing transform police attitudes, organizational culture and role perceptions?
3. Does conferencing produce conflict-reducing outcomes by helping to solve ongoing problems and reduce recidivism?
4. Will victims, offenders and the community accept a police-based restorative justice response?
5. How does the introduction of conferencing alter the case processing of juvenile offenders?
6. How does conferencing compare to the existing system and to victim-offender mediation?

1. Can typical American police officers conduct conferences consistent with due process and restorative justice principles?

To safeguard due process in conferences, facilitators are instructed to let offenders know they have the right to leave the conference at any stage and have the matter referred to formal adjudication should they wish to exercise their rights against self-incrimination or to legal counsel. Officers explicitly included this statement in 50 of the 56 conferences observed. Ninety-two percent of conferenced offenders and 96 percent of conferenced victims indicated it was their own choice to participate. The fact that a majority of offenders declined to participate also demonstrates that the police-based conferencing was voluntary. Therefore, offenders were informed of their right to leave and understood that they had a right to a court appearance if they chose.

Without adequate training and supervision, some officers tended toward authoritarian behavior patterns and may have undermined the process of reintegrative shaming. Conference facilitators need to realize the importance that all participants fully understand the strictly voluntary nature of their participation and that the terms of conference agreements are up to the participants alone.

Victims also have the right to leave the conference process at any stage and to pursue their case in court, although this is not explicitly stated as part of conference facilitator protocol. Nevertheless, 96 percent of victims said that participating in the conference was their own choice. The fact that 4 percent of victims may have felt some coercion to participate is a concern. Perhaps instructing facilitators to ensure that victims understand this prior to the conference and including a statement about the victim's right to leave during the conference would further decrease the chance that victims would feel coerced into participating. It appears from the responses to the surveys that offenders and victims who felt some coercion to participate were feeling that pressure from their family members and not from the facilitating officers.

The issue of disproportionate outcomes from conferences is worthy of examination. To some degree, comparing conference outcomes to court outcomes is like comparing apples and oranges. Courts are largely geared toward requiring offenders to pay fines and costs, and only sometimes requiring restitution or other reparative actions. Conferences are geared toward facilitating a mutually acceptable agreement that often involves community service, apologies and other creative solutions. The community service hours assigned offenders in conferences were often high, compared to what is normally assigned for similar crimes in district courts. In courts, monetary payments are more common than community service, and when community service is assigned, it is of less duration than that assigned in conferences.

Some officers showed a better understanding of restorative justice principles than others. It should be noted, however, that the training that these officers received did not include explicit instruction on the tenets of restorative justice. The current REAL JUSTICE® training process does to a greater extent (REAL JUSTICE® trainer manual as of 7/25/97). Restoration and reparation replace punishment in the restorative justice model. Most facilitators adequately explained that the purpose of the conference was to repair the harm and let participants decide what they wanted to see happen. Some facilitators, however, asked questions such as "What do you think is an appropriate punishment?" or "How much community service would like to see done?" when participants hadn't mentioned community service. The tendency to affect conference agreements is clearly a deviation from the intended purpose of the conference, which is to encourage participants to come up with their own reparative solutions.

Some officers also engaged in lecturing of offenders about the wrongs and ill effects of crime. This is inappropriate in a conference, where the officer plays a facilitative role in encouraging those who were personally affected to let the offender know the offense was wrong and how it was harmful. Such lecturing can be perceived as stigmatizing and have negative effects. Analysis in Chapter 3 suggested that facilitator adherence to protocol and non-authoritarian behavior is positively related to offender remorse, offender perceptions of reintegration, fairness and accountability, as well as victim satisfaction and forgiveness.

There was some evidence to suggest that, after facilitators received feedback on conferences during an in-service training, they began conducting conferences in a more restorative manner. Ongoing feedback to ensure that facilitators are conducting conferences in accordance with protocol may be necessary, especially where the police department as a whole is not sympathetic to a restorative, problem-solving approach.

Regarding the concern that police officers would not be sufficiently prepared for conferences, significantly inhibiting the chances of meaningful exchange and resolution, this generally did not appear to be the case. It was evident that a few officers were ill-prepared and occasionally discouraged emotional exchange during conferences. For many of the retail theft conferences, it is doubtful that more substantial preparation would have enhanced the emotionality of the conferences. For some of the cases involving more personal victimization, more preparation would have been preferable and could have enhanced the quality of the conferences, although participant satisfaction was unrelated to conference preparation.

Young offenders did on some occasions seem to be intimidated by all the adults in the conference. Whether the police officer facilitated the conference in uniform did not appear to have an effect. Facilitators did not make sufficient efforts to invite members of the offender's peer group, in order to encourage the offender to feel safer to open up and express thoughts and feelings. More preparation of the offender may have helped in encouraging offenders to participate more fully in conferences.

The scripted conferencing process seemed generally acceptable to participants, regardless of ethnicity. In several conferences where there were participants who did not understand or speak English proficiently, translators were present. These translators were mostly members of the non-English-speaking person's family. Facilitators could have been more sensitive to the need to alter the process slightly so that proper translation could occur.

In general, officers did a sufficient but not exemplary job in adhering to principles of restorative justice and ensuring due process. In spite of this, participants overwhelmingly said they were satisfied with how their cases were handled, they perceived the process as fair, they would choose to do the conference again, and they would recommend conferences to others. These results should lay to rest the belief that police-based conferencing cannot be implemented in the Unites States, or that American police cannot conduct conferences consistent with restorative principles. These results, which are consistent with earlier evaluations of police conferencing in Australia, lend support to the generalizability of the Australian findings to the United States.

2. Does conferencing transform police attitudes, organizational culture and role perceptions?

The police surveys show there were no significant changes in overall police attitudes, organizational culture or role perceptions as the result of 18 police officers conducting conferences in the Bethlehem Police Department over the year-and-a-half of the experiment. This is contrary to conclusions reached on the conferencing program in Wagga Wagga, New South Wales, Australia, which suggested that involvement in conferencing produced a cultural shift from a punitive legalistic approach to a more problem-solving, restorative approach (Moore, 1995).

It is likely that the lack of a department-wide change in attitudes is due to the marginalization of the conferencing program in Bethlehem. Facilitating conferences was not an organizational priority. Evidence suggests that officers and supervisors saw conferencing as an extra task which interfered with and took time from patrol and responding to calls for service. Officers were not given sufficient support from line supervisors to make adequate preparations for conferences. There was support from administration, but while this support is important, real change cannot occur without support from supervisors who oversee the day-to-day activities of officers. If officers were to seriously rethink their views of policing, the effect of exposure to conferencing would have to be complemented with sufficient organizational and managerial support. Otherwise, as shown in this experiment, it is business as usual.

The program in Wagga Wagga had more support from the department as a whole. The program was integrated into the everyday operations of the department, with a sergeants review panel who selected cases and oversaw the facilitation of conferences. Additionally, the process of developing and implementing the program involved more input from the police department as a whole. This is dramatically different from the program in Bethlehem, which was implemented in a "bottom-up" fashion with support from top administration. As of the end of this experiment, the Bethlehem Police Department is in the process of implementing a standard operating procedure for juvenile diversionary conferences and will include supervisory responsibilities for the sergeants. It will remain to be seen if this effort will sufficiently integrate conferencing into everyday operations and if such an integration will eventually produce a shift in the police culture.

It is possible that the minimal amount of exposure to conferencing and the types of cases dealt with in Bethlehem were responsible for the slight impact of the conferencing program on individual officers. Those officers who were involved in conferencing only conducted a few conferences over the 18-month experimental period, making it unlikely that the positive effects of these conferences could have made a significant impact on their attitudes toward policing generally. Also, most of the conferences dealt with retail thefts and were not very dramatic in demonstrating the restorative possibilities of conferences. Because the victims in the majority of conferences were store representatives and the harm of these offenses are somewhat abstract, there was less dramatic reintegration of offenders. Forgiveness by these victims carried less emotional impact than was evident with the victims of violent offenses. Perhaps if officers were consistently exposed to conferences that successfully dealt with more serious instances of offending and victimization, they would be more inclined to change their attitudes about policing and more favorably disposed to a restorative response.

This lack of a significant change in police culture is very similar to that seen in numerous evaluations of community policing programs across the United States. While there have been isolated incidents of successes of community policing, attempts to implement community policing have been largely limited to specialized units of officers and have not permeated the command-and-control functions of everyday police work (Couper & Loubitz, 1991). Factors working against the implementation of community policing are traditional police norms (Skolnick & Bayley, 1988; Weisburd, McElroy & Hardyman, 1988; Nelligan & Taylor, 1994); police organizational and subcultural resistance (Rosenbaum & Lurigio, 1994; Gaines, 1994; Overman, Carey & Dolan, 1994; Walker, 1993; Goldstein, 1987); and lack of support from middle management (Zhao, Thurman & Lovrich, 1995; Overman, Carey & Dolan, 1994; Walker, 1993; Riechers & Roberg, 1990; Goldstein, 1987; Koch & Bennett, 1993; Redlinger, 1994). These factors all appear to be present in the Bethlehem study and represent obstacles for the system-wide implementation of restorative policing.

The police culture and organizational climate must be compatible for community policing to be successful (Lurigio & Skogan, 1994). It appears from the results of the attitudinal and occupational surveys conducted in the present study that officers who are more supportive of the notions of community and problem-oriented policing will also be supportive of restorative approaches to policing. It was the case in the present study that those officers who are not supportive of conferencing are also those most likely to oppose community policing approaches. Thus, it seems likely that the whole effect of conferencing was to cause a few officers who were positively disposed to community policing to become more supportive of such approaches.

3. Does conferencing produce conflict-reducing outcomes by helping to solve ongoing problems and reduce recidivism?

The low rates of recidivism for violent offenses suggests that conferencing helps reduce or resolve conflict. The universal ability of conference participants to come up with mutually acceptable agreements also implies that conferences are useful in facilitating a collective, community-based solution to these criminal problems. The ongoing acceptability of these solutions are supported by the overwhelming satisfaction and perceptions of fairness on the part of victims, offenders and parents of offenders as reported in survey responses. The 94 percent voluntary compliance with the terms of the agreements also supports the conclusion that these criminal conflicts were resolved in a manner satisfactory to all participants.

With regard to recidivism, the evidence is not conclusive. It appears that any reductions in recidivism are the result of conferencing selecting out those juveniles who are least likely to re-offend in the first place. Future studies will be necessary to determine whether the lower recidivism of participating offenders is due to the conflict-reducing nature of the conferencing process, an increase in offender empathy or a self-selection effect.

In addition to the strong evidence of a self-selection bias in the types of offenders willing to participate in police conferencing, the long-term outcomes of conferencing on future re-offending differs greatly by crime type. The much lower rearrest rate for violent offenders suggests that conferencing did result in a reduction of conflict for the individuals involved in these cases.

4. Will victims, offenders and the community accept a police-based restorative justice response?

Victims, offenders and parents of offenders were consistently satisfied with the conferencing process and perceived the process and the outcomes as fair, even more so than formal adjudication. Nearly all respondents indicated they would choose to participate in the program again and would recommend it to others facing similar trouble. Thus, for those participating in conferencing, the overwhelming support for police-based conferencing was evident from the data.

The concern expressed by some critics of police-based conferencing that the police should not run conferences because of the coercive nature of policing appears to be largely unfounded and may be based upon a stereotyped vision of policing. Policing has undergone a significant shift toward a more problem-solving approach in recent years. However, there was a tendency by some officers early in the program to use an authoritarian posture and this concern cannot be dismissed entirely. Some officers appear to have had problems using a nondirective style, and this may be more a function of individual officers' (mis)perception of their roles. Those officers who were most supportive of a service-oriented community policing approach were also supportive of conferencing for juveniles.

The concern raised by some critics of police-run conferences that police do not enjoy the respect of young people may be a bit of a "chicken-and-egg" issue. There was some resistance to participating in conferences, but no more than that found in studies of mediation programs using community volunteers. In fact, participation rates were higher in the present study than for any of the mediation programs considered. The fact that participation rates were as high for Hispanic offenders as it was for white offenders, and that conferences requiring translators were as positively received as those without, demonstrates that the police in Bethlehem do have the respect of a majority of residents. The lower participation rate for black offenders in the study suggests that for this minority group, police are not as trusted as they are for other residents. However, given the small number of blacks selected for the study, no definitive conclusion can be reached in this regard.

It is clear from the high satisfaction and sense of fairness of victims, offenders and offender's parents participating in conferencing that the community not only accepts a police-based restorative justice process, but that they find it more fair and just than traditional court processes.

5. How does the introduction of conferencing alter the case processing of juvenile offenders?

Conferencing did not appear to alter the way in which juvenile offenders were processed and disposed. The police disposition of cases did not change as a result of the experiment. Cases were successfully diverted without net-widening effects. Dispositions of cases handled by court was substantially unchanged after the introduction of diversionary conferences.

Offenders who agree to participate had a lower risk of rearrest than offenders declining to participate. Offenders participating in the study were those most likely to have pled guilty and were less likely to have been fined had they gone to court. It remains a possibility that the small proportion of all juvenile cases diverted through conferencing was insufficient to produce a change in court processing. If the proportion of all juvenile cases diverted was greater, those cases remaining in the formal system may be qualitatively different, and this could eventually produce a detectable process effect on remaining court cases.

For the types of cases eligible for police-based diversion, there was no apparent effect on court processing of cases not included in the study. The introduction of police-based conferences into the existing system at the level in the present study had no discernible downstream processing effect on cases not included.

An ideal diversion programs would have a number of characteristics. It 1) would actually divert cases from further formal processing, 2) would occur as early in the justice system as possible, 3) would divert those offenders who have the lowest risk of reoffense, and 4) would satisfy the victim-complainant. Additionally, an ideal diversion program would also be respectful of offenders, empowering of their families and positive social supporters, and provide an important lesson in accountability for everyone involved, i.e. to be restorative. Thus it appears that police-based conferencing has the characteristics of an ideal diversion program.

6. How does conferencing compare to the existing system and to other restorative justice programs?

We were surprised by the high degree of satisfaction expressed by victims, offenders and offender's parents with the traditional criminal justice response to their case. Offenders whose cases were processed by the magistrate court were satisfied with how their case was handled in 96 percent of the control cases and 87 percent of the decline cases. While the proportion of offenders who rated court as very satisfying was not as high as those attending a conference, offender satisfaction with court was higher than in all of the aforementioned studies of victim-offender mediation. The development of the lay magistrate court was intended to create a justice process that was more informal and responsive to the needs of individual cases than traditional juvenile court. The results of this study demonstrate that offenders and their parents were generally satisfied with these community courts. An overwhelming proportion of offenders felt that their case was handled fairly and that the process was fair to themselves and their victims, regardless of whether their case was handled by the existing system or by a police-run conference.

Police-based conferences produced outcomes for offenders more specifically tailored to the individual's circumstances than the court process, especially for violent cases with personal victims. Conference participants were more likely to agree to community service as a reparative response and less likely to agree to monetary payments than imposed by the existing system. This may be largely a function of the resources available to the magistrate court, but police-based restorative responses appear to be more flexible and adaptable than the court process.

Victims and offenders participating in conferences had higher satisfaction and perceptions of fairness than in victim-offender mediation programs. Both conferencing and mediation had higher satisfaction and perceptions of fairness than their respective court-comparison groups. How much these differences can be attributed to the voluntary programs themselves, and how much can be attributed to more cooperative cases choosing to participate remains an open question.

Limitations of the current study

There were a number of substantive research issues raised by the Bethlehem experiment. The first is that crime type matters. The effect of conferencing was quite different for violent cases than for property cases, and researchers should block their survey designs by at least this minimum distinction. Future research should also include the nature of the victim as a factor in their sampling frames.

The support for restorative policing within police departments remains an open question. Given the moderate response of police officers to surveys generally and the large attrition rate this produces, a matched-cases design will always be limited. However, without it, this study might have concluded (falsely) that the department had changed in measured attitudes by comparing aggregate means at the two time periods. Anonymous questionnaires might have improved the response rate slightly at the cost of important statistical power. The response rate in this study was as good as those reported for other anonymous police surveys. Thus, the promise of confidentiality without anonymity was sufficient to produce unbiased matched pre-test/post-test samples.

Another important research implication is that voluntary restorative police-based diversionary programs produce a strong self-selection bias. Future research should attempt to identify factors that distinguish the sample of the willing from the unwilling. More work needs to explore what might be possible to bring a restorative response to cases involving uncooperative offenders, for the sake of their victims and communities, perhaps in collaboration with probation departments.

Experimental studies on restorative justice programs need to include a very large number of subjects. Because uncooperative cases are less likely to participate, future experimental studies of restorative programs should have a large enough sample so that some of the self-selection factors can be used as control variables in a multivariate approach. In experiments that randomize only participating cases, the number of cases needs to be large enough to detect statistical significance with small differences at the extreme ends of the scales.

There is no such thing as a perfect research design. Every experiment is prone to various threats to internal and external validity. The present study used a blocked randomized post-test-only design (in the case assignment part of the experiment). This is the same design as RISE. The difference between RISE and the present study is the point of case sampling. RISE is randomizing cases referred by the arresting officer at the point after the offender has already agreed to participate.

The present study randomized cases whose case profile fit the established criteria, before anyone had been given information about the program. Thus, this study sampled "typical" types of such cases handled by the police in Bethlehem. The sampling frame in RISE is a subset of typical cases—offenders who have chosen to participate and whose cases were referred by the arresting officer. It remains to be seen how representative that sampling frame is of typical cases handled by the police in Canberra.

RISE will be in a stronger position to assert comparability between treatment and control groups. This should allow for a stronger analysis of program effects, since the program effects will not be as "contaminated" with self-selection effects as the present study. Presumably, RISE's control and treatment groups have been subjected to equal amounts of these effects. However, the presence of self-selection effects in voluntary programs like the Australian National Police diversionary conferencing program are not removed, only held constant. The RISE study can determine how the program affects only on the kinds of cases that are predisposed to be cooperative and have low recidivism. Because all of the cases in RISE are predisposed to be cooperative, it is expected that the control cases will be equally predisposed. Thus, RISE will be looking for program effects among cases predisposed to be satisfied and have low recidivism. RISE will be facing the problem of finding significance between low and lower recidivism, or between high and higher satisfaction. The lack of significant program effects at the margins would not demonstrate the actual lack of program effects, only that these effects could not be demonstrated at the margins. Only very large samples can achieve statistical significance under such circumstances.

The present study was more interested in measuring the effects of the pilot program on the police department, on typical offenders and their victims and parents, and on the rest of the system. This was the first evaluation of police-based conferencing in the United States. The available literature suggested that American police would not be able to abandon their authoritarian role and empower communities to determine outcomes—and that communities would not trust the police to be helpful. It was important to establish a true participation rate for the Bethlehem Police FGC project to address these concerns.

Umbreit's mediation evaluations reported the number of cases mediated as well as the total number of cases referred to the program; computing the program participation rate is straightforward. There is every reason to expect that the sampling frame of cases where victim and offender agree to mediation suffers from the same self-selection effects as the present study. The nature and magnitude of this bias is unknown for the mediation studies and could account for some of the differences in comparisons. The present research suggests that such cases probably had higher satisfaction and lower recidivism than their respective declining cases, even if the programs were no better than courts.

Both the VOM studies and RISE are prone to an additional threat to external validity. Cases are referred by justice professionals at their discretion. Differences between referred cases and typical cases are unknown and unaccounted for in the research designs. RISE will attempt to assess the magnitude of the referral bias in a "pipeline" study, which should provide some interesting results.

Documenting the self-selection effect may be one of the present study's unique contributions to the accumulating empirical knowledge about restorative justice programs. It is likely that a very strong case self-selection effect will be present in all voluntary programs, whether it is controlled for (as in RISE) or not (as in VOM and the present study). This represents a major obstacle to all restorative justice research. If representative cases are sampled, internal validity is threatened; if only participating cases are sampled, external validity is threatened. In the former, positive results should be expected even when there is no program effect; in the latter, differences among pre-selected cooperative cases must be demonstrated, and even then the generalizability of the results will remain unknown.

This study did not find that police-based conferencing <u>produced</u> higher participant satisfaction or lower recidivism than the traditional system. It found that <u>participants</u> in conferences had higher satisfaction and lower recidivism than participants in the traditional system. Factors associated with the decision to participate were related to factors associated with the outcome variables. The design in this study allowed for the demonstration of the effect, but not the disentanglement of the selection and program effects.

There was only one statistically significant program effect between conferencing and court regarding satisfaction or recidivism. Among property victims, the treatment group was more likely than the control group to feel the offender was held accountable. Thus, retail store managers felt conferencing held offenders accountable more often than court. In all other respects, conferencing outcomes were no better than court outcomes, beyond the effects resulting from cooperative cases agreeing to participate and problematic cases declining.

Limiting definitions of program success to recidivism, participation and satisfaction rates is insufficient to evaluate restorative justice programs. Diversionary restorative programs provide offenders who are willing to admit their wrongdoing and face up to their victims with an option to be held accountable without an official court record. The restorative option also provides the opportunity for victims, offenders' parents, and their respective communities to play central roles in determining the resolution of the case. These are worthy accomplishments in themselves.

Where communities affected by a crime can voluntarily resolve such cases to their own satisfaction, they should be encouraged to do so. Police-based diversionary conferences provide the communities with this possibility. Courts are better equipped to respond to the remaining 58% of cases where the affected parties cannot voluntarily agree on reparation terms, as is their charge. The trend in restorative justice toward a bifurcated justice system will likely be increased due to the presence of a strong self-selection effect.

The randomized experimental part of this study has implications for two of the six research questions addressed. Regardless of the internal validity of that part of the experiment, the other results remain valid. This study demonstrated that U.S. police can be trained to handle the first-time juvenile cases when the parties involved want a restorative option. The Bethlehem Family Group Conferencing Program produced participation rates and participant satisfaction as high as other well regarded restorative justice programs. It remains to be seen what restorative practices can be effective with more serious offenses, with adult offenders, or with uncooperative offenders and their affected communities.

General Conclusions

In summary, the following general conclusions can be made:

- Typical American police officers are capable of conducting conferences consistent with due process and restorative justice principles.
- While conferencing did not transform police attitudes, organization culture or role perceptions, it did move those with the most exposure to conferencing toward a more community-oriented, problem-solving stance.
- Conferencing can produce conflict-reducing outcomes, most clearly in cases of interpersonal violence. Because of a strong self-selection bias, this study could not confirm a reduction in recidivism due to conferencing. Like other voluntary diversion programs, cooperative cases participated, uncooperative cases did not.
- Victims, offenders and parents who participated almost universally accepted this police-based restorative justice response, as indicated by high rates of satisfaction with the process and experiences of fairness.
- Conferencing proved to be an ideal early diversionary approach, diverting those offenders least likely to re-offend while avoiding net-widening.
- Police-facilitated restorative conferences produced higher satisfaction, perceptions of fairness and participation rates for less cost than victim-offender mediation programs.
- Conferencing effectively motivates offenders to the extent that they almost universally complete financial reparation, community service, apologies and other obligations to victims.

Appendices

		pages
Appendix 1	Family Group Conference Data Sheet	116-117
Appendix 2	Post Conference Offender Questionnaire	118-119
Appendix 3	Post Conference Victim Questionnaire	120-121
Appendix 4	Post Conference Parent Questionnaire	122-123
Appendix 5	Offender (Court) Questionnaire	124
Appendix 6	Victim (Court) Questionnaire	125
Appendix 7	Parent (Court) Questionnaire	126-127
Appendix 8	Conference Observation Sheet	128-129
Appendix 9	Police Attitude Scales and Items	130-136

FAMILY GROUP CONFERENCE DATA SHEET

Date of conference: ___/___/___   Date of offense: ___/___/___

(Please provide the following information on all FGCs conducted and return this form in the attached envelope to REAL JUSTICE, P.O. Box 229, Bethlehem, PA 18016. YOUR PARTICIPATION IS IMPORTANT! Thank you.)

Program Site: _____

Name of coordinator: _____

Nature of offense: _____

Description of offense: _____

_____

_____

_____

Name of primary offender (or case number): _____

Were the victim(s) and offender(s) acquainted before the offense?
☐ yes   ☐ no

IF YES: How were they known to each other?
☐ friend   ☐ acquaintance   ☐ neighbor   ☐ other: specify _____

Who was present at the conference?

number of offenders: ____   number of victims: ____

number of offender supporters: ____   number of victim supporters: ____

total number of participants (excluding yourself): ____

Was a formal agreement signed?   ☐ yes   ☐ no   (IF YES, attach a copy)

Was a formal apology offered?   ☐ yes   ☐ no

How would you rate this conference process?
☐ very positive   ☐ positive   ☐ mixed   ☐ negative   ☐ very negative

How would you rate this conference outcome?
☐ very positive   ☐ positive   ☐ mixed   ☐ negative   ☐ very negative

Would you say the tone of the conference was generally
☐ friendly   ☐ hostile   ☐ other: specify: _____

How long did this conference take? (hours : minutes) ____ : ____

Not counting the time of the conference itself, how much time did you spend preparing for the conference? (hours : minutes) ____ : ____

How would you rate your experience from 1 (horrible) to 10 (ecstatic)? ____

ADDITIONAL COMMENTS:
(e.g., offender parents difficult, victim found healing, offender refused responsibility, etc.)

PARTICIPANT DATA SHEET

Age of offender #____: _____
- [ ] male [ ] female
- [ ] white [ ] black [ ] Hispanic
- [ ] other (specify): _____

Age of offender #____: _____
- [ ] male [ ] female
- [ ] white [ ] black [ ] Hispanic
- [ ] other (specify): _____

Age of offender #____: _____
- [ ] male [ ] female
- [ ] white [ ] black [ ] Hispanic
- [ ] other (specify): _____

Age of victim #____: _____
- [ ] male [ ] female
- [ ] white [ ] black [ ] Hispanic
- [ ] other (specify): _____

Age of victim #____: _____
- [ ] male [ ] female
- [ ] white [ ] black [ ] Hispanic
- [ ] other (specify): _____

Age of victim #____: _____
- [ ] male [ ] female
- [ ] white [ ] black [ ] Hispanic
- [ ] other (specify): _____

Check all offender supporters present:

Offender #_____
- [ ] both parents
- [ ] mother only
- [ ] father only
- [ ] siblings (number: _____)
- [ ] other relative (specify): _____
- [ ] other relative (specify): _____
- [ ] other non-relative (specify): _____
- [ ] other non-relative (specify): _____

Offender #_____
- [ ] both parents
- [ ] mother only
- [ ] father only
- [ ] siblings (number: _____)
- [ ] other relative (specify): _____
- [ ] other relative (specify): _____
- [ ] other non-relative (specify): _____
- [ ] other non-relative (specify): _____

Offender #_____
- [ ] both parents
- [ ] mother only
- [ ] father only
- [ ] siblings (number: _____)
- [ ] other relative (specify): _____
- [ ] other relative (specify): _____
- [ ] other non-relative (specify): _____
- [ ] other non-relative (specify): _____

Check all victim supporters present:

Victim #_____
- [ ] both parents
- [ ] mother only
- [ ] father only
- [ ] siblings (number: _____)
- [ ] other relative (specify): _____
- [ ] other relative (specify): _____
- [ ] other non-relative (specify): _____
- [ ] other non-relative (specify): _____

Victim #_____
- [ ] both parents
- [ ] mother only
- [ ] father only
- [ ] siblings (number: _____)
- [ ] other relative (specify): _____
- [ ] other relative (specify): _____
- [ ] other non-relative (specify): _____
- [ ] other non-relative (specify): _____

Victim #_____
- [ ] both parents
- [ ] mother only
- [ ] father only
- [ ] siblings (number: _____)
- [ ] other relative (specify): _____
- [ ] other relative (specify): _____
- [ ] other non-relative (specify): _____
- [ ] other non-relative (specify): _____

USE ADDITIONAL FORMS IF NECESSARY. REPRODUCE AND ATTACH.

POST CONFERENCE OFFENDER QUESTIONNAIRE

Date of conference: ___/___/___   Today's date: ___/___/___

(Please indicate your answer to the following questions and return this form in the attached envelope to Cpt. Stahr, Bethlehem Police Department, 10 E. Church Street, Bethlehem, PA 18018. YOUR OPINION MATTERS! Thank you.)

1. How satisfied were you with the way your case was handled?
   ___ very satisfied   ___ satisfied   ___ dissatisfied   ___ very dissatisfied

3. Do you feel that being in the conference was your own choice?
   ___ yes   ___ yes, but under pressure   ___ no

   3a. IF YES: Why did you choose to participate in the Family Group Conference program?
   ___ to pay back the victim(s) for their losses   ___ to let the victim(s) know why I did it
   ___ to help the victim(s)   ___ to offer an apology
   ___ to take direct responsibility for making things right
   ___ other: specify _____

4. Would you say the tone of the conference was generally
   ___ friendly   ___ hostile   ___ other: specify _____

5. Did you apologize to the victim(s) for what you did?   ___ yes   ___ no

6. Was it helpful to meet with the victim(s) in a conference setting?
   ___ not at all helpful   ___ somewhat helpful   ___ very helpful

7. Were you surprised by anything that occurred in the conference session?   ___ yes   ___ no

   7a. IF YES: By what?
   ___ it went better than I expected   ___ the victim(s) seemed to care about me
   ___ it was worse than I expected   ___ the victim(s) was so angry
   ___ other: specify _____

8. For the following, please indicate how important each item was to you during the conference:

   To be able to tell the victim(s) what happened.
   ___ very important   ___ important   ___ unimportant   ___ very unimportant

   To pay back the victim(s) by paying them money or doing some work.
   ___ very important   ___ important   ___ unimportant   ___ very unimportant

   To have the opportunity to work out an agreement with the victim(s) that was acceptable to both of us.
   ___ very important   ___ important   ___ unimportant   ___ very unimportant

   To be able to apologize to the victim(s) for what I did.
   ___ very important   ___ important   ___ unimportant   ___ very unimportant

   To be able to apologize to my family and friends for what I did.
   ___ very important   ___ important   ___ unimportant   ___ very unimportant

9. Was a repayment or community service agreement negotiated during the conference?   ___ yes   ___ no

   9a. IF YES: Was the agreement fair to you?   ___ yes   ___ no
   Was the agreement fair to the victim(s)?   ___ yes   ___ no

10. Which of the following best describes your attitude toward the victim(s) now?
    ___ very positive   ___ positive   ___ mixed   ___ negative   ___ very negative

11. Do you think the victim(s) has a better opinion of you after the conference?   ___ yes   ___ no

12. Do you think your family/friends have a better opinion of you after the conference?   ___ yes   ___ no

13. How likely do you think it is that you will commit another similar offense?
    ___ very likely   ___ likely   ___ unlikely   ___ very unlikely

14. Which of the following best describes your attitude about the conferencing session?
    ☐ very positive   ☐ positive   ☐ mixed   ☐ negative   ☐ very negative
15. If you had it to do over again, would you choose to participate in a Family Group Conference?
    ☐ yes   ☐ no
16. Would you recommend Family Group Conferencing to other friends who might get in trouble?
    ☐ yes   ☐ no
17. Do you believe that your opinion regarding the offense and circumstances was adequately considered in this case?   ☐ yes   ☐ no
18. Given your understanding of fairness, did you experience fairness in your case?   ☐ yes   ☐ no

19. Of the following items, please rank the 3 most important concerns you have related to fairness in the system when kids do something wrong, with #1 being the most important.

    rank

    ___ punishing the offender

    ___ paying back the victim

    ___ getting help for the offender

    ___ having the offender personally make things right

    ___ allowing the offender to apologize to the victim

    ___ allowing the offender to apologize to their family

    ___ other: specify _____

20. The following represent statements that are sometimes made by people in trouble who participate in Family Group Conferences. Please mark whether you agree or disagree with each statement.

    Too much pressure was put on me to do all the talking in the conference.
       ☐ strongly agree   ☐ agree   ☐ disagree   ☐ strongly disagree
    I felt I had no choice about participating in the conference with my victim(s).
       ☐ strongly agree   ☐ agree   ☐ disagree   ☐ strongly disagree
    The victim(s) was not sincere in his/her participation.
       ☐ strongly agree   ☐ agree   ☐ disagree   ☐ strongly disagree
    I have a better understanding of how my behavior affected the victim(s).
       ☐ strongly agree   ☐ agree   ☐ disagree   ☐ strongly disagree
    The victim(s) participated only because he/she wanted the money back or to be paid for damages.
       ☐ strongly agree   ☐ agree   ☐ disagree   ☐ strongly disagree
    Conferences make the justice process more responsive to my needs as a human being.
       ☐ strongly agree   ☐ agree   ☐ disagree   ☐ strongly disagree
    Without Family Group Conferences I probably would have gotten punished much worse.
       ☐ strongly agree   ☐ agree   ☐ disagree   ☐ strongly disagree

21. Is there anything else you would like to say about the Family Group Conference session or about how your case was handled?

POST CONFERENCE VICTIM QUESTIONNAIRE

Date of conference: ___/___/___　　　　　　　　　　　　　　　Today's date: ___/___/___

(Please indicate your answer to the following questions and return this form to Cpt. Stahr, Bethlehem Police Department, 10 E. Church Street, Bethlehem, PA 18018. YOUR OPINION MATTERS! Thank you.)

1. Did you know the offender before the offense occurred?　___ yes　___ no
    - if multiple offenders:　___ knew all　___ knew one or more　___ knew none
    - 1a. IF YES: How did you know the offender? if multiple offenders, check all that apply
        - ___ friend　___ acquaintance　___ neighbor　___ other: specify _____

2. Of the following possible effects of the offense on your life, which one was the most important for you?
    - ___ a greater sense of fear
    - ___ the loss of property
    - ___ the damage to property
    - ___ a feeling of powerlessness
    - ___ the hassle of dealing with police and court officials

3. How satisfied were you with the way the system handled your case?
    - ___ very satisfied　___ satisfied　___ dissatisfied　___ very dissatisfied

4. Do you believe that your opinion regarding the offense and offender(s) was adequately considered in this case?
    - ___ yes　___ no

5. Do you believe the offender was adequately held accountable for his/her behavior?　___ yes　___ no
    - if multiple offenders:　___ all were held accountable　___ one or more were held accountable　___ none were

6. Do you believe that Family Group Conferencing should be offered, on a voluntary basis, to all victims?　___ yes　___ no

7. Do you feel that being in the conference was your own choice?
    - ___ yes　___ yes, but under pressure　___ no
    - 7a. IF YES: Why did you choose to participate in the Family Group Conference program?
        - ___ to get paid back for losses
        - ___ to receive answers to questions I had
        - ___ to help the offender(s)
        - ___ to receive an apology
        - ___ to let the offender(s) know how I felt about the offense
        - ___ other: specify _____

8. Would you say the tone of the conference was generally
    - ___ friendly　___ hostile　___ other: specify _____

9. Were you surprised by anything that occurred in the conference session?　___ yes　___ no
    - 9a. IF YES: By what?
        - ___ it went better than I expected
        - ___ the offender(s) seemed sincere
        - ___ it was worse than I expected
        - ___ the offender(s) was arrogant
        - ___ other: specify _____

10. Did the offender seem to be sorry about the way he/she hurt you?　___ yes　___ no
    - if multiple offenders:　___ all seemed sorry　___ one or more seemed sorry　___ none seemed sorry

11. Did the offender offer an apology?　___ yes　___ no
    - if multiple offenders:　___ all apologized　___ one or more apologized　___ none apologized

12. Was it helpful to meet the offender(s) in the conference setting?
    - ___ not at all helpful　___ somewhat helpful　___ very helpful

13. Was a restitution or community service agreement negotiated during the conference?　___ yes　___ no
    - 13a. IF YES: Was the agreement fair to you?　___ yes　___ no
    - Was the agreement fair to the offender?　___ yes　___ no
    - if multiple offenders:　___ fair to all　___ fair to one or more　___ fair to none

14. How likely do you think it is that the offender will commit a similar offense against somebody?
    - ___ very likely　___ likely　___ unlikely　___ very unlikely
    - if multiple offenders:　likely for ___ offender(s)　unlikely for ___ offender(s)

15. Would you recommend Family Group Conferencing to other victims? ☐ yes ☐ no
16. Given your understanding of fairness, did you experience fairness in your case? ☐ yes ☐ no
17. For the following, please indicate how important each item was to you during the conference:

    To receive answers to questions I wanted to ask the offender(s).
    ☐ very important ☐ important ☐ unimportant ☐ very unimportant

    To tell the offender(s) how the offense affected me.
    ☐ very important ☐ important ☐ unimportant ☐ very unimportant

    To get paid back for my losses by the offender(s).
    ☐ very important ☐ important ☐ unimportant ☐ very unimportant

    To see that the offender(s) got come counseling or other type of help.
    ☐ very important ☐ important ☐ unimportant ☐ very unimportant

    To have the offender(s) punished.
    ☐ very important ☐ important ☐ unimportant ☐ very unimportant

    To have the offender(s) say he or she is sorry.
    ☐ very important ☐ important ☐ unimportant ☐ very unimportant

    To have the opportunity to negotiate a repayment agreement with the offender(s) that was acceptable to both of us.
    ☐ very important ☐ important ☐ unimportant ☐ very unimportant

18. If you had it to do over again, would you choose to participate in a Family Group Conference?
    ☐ yes ☐ no

19. The following represent statements that are sometimes made by victims who participate in Family Group Conferences. Please indicate whether you agree or disagree with each statement.

    Family Group Conferencing allowed me to express my feelings about being victimized.
    ☐ strongly agree ☐ agree ☐ disagree ☐ strongly disagree

    Family Group Conferencing allowed me to participate more fully in the system.
    ☐ strongly agree ☐ agree ☐ disagree ☐ strongly disagree

    The offender(s) was not sincere in his/her participation.
    ☐ strongly agree ☐ agree ☐ disagree ☐ strongly disagree

    I have a better understanding of why the offense was committed against me.
    ☐ strongly agree ☐ agree ☐ disagree ☐ strongly disagree

    The offender(s) participated only because he/she was trying to avoid punishment.
    ☐ strongly agree ☐ agree ☐ disagree ☐ strongly disagree

    Conferences make the justice process more responsive to my needs as a human being.
    ☐ strongly agree ☐ agree ☐ disagree ☐ strongly disagree

20. Of the following items, please rank the 3 most important concerns you have related to fairness in the system, with #1 being the most important.

    rank
    ____ punishing the offender
    ____ paying back the victim
    ____ getting help for the offender
    ____ having the offender personally make things right
    ____ actively participating in the process
    ____ receiving the offender's expression of apology
    ____ other: specify_____

21. Is there anything else you would like to say about the Family Group Conference session with your offender(s) or about how your case was handled?

case# _____ **POST CONFERENCE PARENT'S QUESTIONNAIRE**

Date of conference: ___/___/___   Today's date: ___/___/___

Please indicate your answer to the following questions and return this form in the attached envelope to Cpt. Stahr, Bethlehem Police Department, 10 E. Church Street, Bethlehem, PA 18018. YOUR OPINION MATTERS! Thank you.

1. How satisfied were you with the way your child's case was handled?
   ___ very satisfied ___ satisfied ___ dissatisfied ___ very dissatisfied

2. Do you believe your child was adequately held accountable for the offense committed?
   ___ yes ___ no

3. Was it helpful to meet with the victim(s) in a conference setting?
   ___ not at all helpful ___ somewhat helpful ___ very helpful

4. Were you surprised by anything that occurred in the conference session? ___ yes ___ no
   4a. IF YES: By what?
   ___ it went better than I expected   ___ the victim(s) seemed to care about my child
   ___ it was worse than I expected   ___ the victim(s) was so angry
   ___ other: specify _____

5. For the following, please indicate how important each item was to you during the conference:
   To be able to tell the victim(s) how you felt.
   ___ very important ___ important ___ unimportant ___ very unimportant
   To be able to tell your child how you felt.
   ___ very important ___ important ___ unimportant ___ very unimportant
   To have the opportunity to work out an agreement with the victim(s) that was acceptable to everyone.
   ___ very important ___ important ___ unimportant ___ very unimportant
   To be able to apologize to the victim(s) for what my child did.
   ___ very important ___ important ___ unimportant ___ very unimportant
   To have my child apologize for what he/she did.
   ___ very important ___ important ___ unimportant ___ very unimportant

6. Was a repayment or community service agreement negotiated during the conference? ___ yes ___ no
   6a. IF YES: Was the agreement fair to you? ___ yes ___ no
   Was the agreement fair to your child? ___ yes ___ no
   Was the agreement fair to the victim(s)? ___ yes ___ no

7. Which of the following best describes your attitude toward your child now?
   ___ very positive ___ positive ___ mixed ___ negative ___ very negative

8. Do you think the victim(s) has a better opinion of your child after the conference? ___ yes ___ no

9. Do you have a better opinion of your child after the conference? ___ yes ___ no

10. How likely do you think it is that your child will commit another similar offense?
    ___ very likely ___ likely ___ unlikely ___ very unlikely

11. Which of the following best describes your attitude about the conferencing session?
    ☐ very positive   ☐ positive   ☐ mixed   ☐ negative   ☐ very negative

12. If you had it to do over again, would you choose to participate in a Family Group Conference?
    ☐ yes   ☐ no

13. Would you recommend Family Group Conferencing to others who face similar trouble?
    ☐ yes   ☐ no

14. Do you believe that your opinion regarding the offense and circumstances was adequately considered in this case?   ☐ yes   ☐ no

15. Given your understanding of fairness, did you experience fairness in your case?   ☐ yes   ☐ no

16. Of the following items, please rank the 3 most important concerns you have related to fairness in the system when kids do something wrong, with #1 being the most important.

    rank
    ____ punishing the offender
    ____ paying back the victim
    ____ getting help for the offender
    ____ having the offender personally make things right
    ____ allowing the offender to apologize to the victim
    ____ allowing the offender to apologize to their family
    ____ other: specify _____

17. The following represent statements that are sometimes made by parents of kids in trouble who participate in Family Group Conferences. Please indicate whether you agree or disagree with each statement.

    Too much pressure was put on my child to do all the talking in the conference.
    ☐ strongly agree   ☐ agree   ☐ disagree   ☐ strongly disagree

    My child was treated with respect during the conference.
    ☐ strongly agree   ☐ agree   ☐ disagree   ☐ strongly disagree

    The victim(s) was not sincere in his/her participation.
    ☐ strongly agree   ☐ agree   ☐ disagree   ☐ strongly disagree

    I have a better understanding of how my child's behavior affected the victim(s).
    ☐ strongly agree   ☐ agree   ☐ disagree   ☐ strongly disagree

    The victim(s) participated only because he/she wanted the money back or to be paid for damages.
    ☐ strongly agree   ☐ agree   ☐ disagree   ☐ strongly disagree

    Conferences make the justice process more responsive to my child's needs as a human being.
    ☐ strongly agree   ☐ agree   ☐ disagree   ☐ strongly disagree

    Without Family Group Conferences my child probably would have gotten punished much worse.
    ☐ strongly agree   ☐ agree   ☐ disagree   ☐ strongly disagree

18. Is there anything else you would like to say about the Family Group Conference session or about how your child's case was handled?

    _____
    _____
    _____

OFFENDER QUESTIONNAIRE

(Please indicate your answer to the following questions and return this form in the enclosed envelope to Cpt. Stahr, Bethlehem Police Department, 10 E. Church Street, Bethlehem, PA 18018. YOUR OPINION MATTERS! Thank you.)

Name of offender: _____

Type of offense: _____ today's date _____

Description of offense: _____

age ____ ☐ male ☐ female ☐ white ☐ black ☐ Hispanic ☐ other (specify) ____

How satisfied were you with the way the justice system handled your case?
☐ very satisfied ☐ satisfied ☐ dissatified ☐ very dissatisfied

Do you believe you were adequately held accountable for the offense you committed?
☐ yes ☐ no

For the following items, please indicate if the item is very important, important, unimportant or very unimportant.

To be able to tell the victim what happened.
☐ very important ☐ important ☐ unimportant ☐ very unimportant

To compensate the victim by paying them money or doing some work.
☐ very important ☐ important ☐ unimportant ☐ very unimportant

To have the opportunity to work out an agreement with the victim that is acceptable to both of you.
☐ very important ☐ important ☐ unimportant ☐ very unimportant

To be able to apologize to the victim for what you did.
☐ very important ☐ important ☐ unimportant ☐ very unimportant

Do you think that a meeting with the victim might be helpful?
☐ not at all helpful ☐ somewhat helpful ☐ very helpful

Would you feel nervous about a structured meeting with the victim attended by your friends and family?
☐ yes ☐ no

Which of the following best describes your attitude toward the victim at this point in time?
☐ very positive ☐ positive ☐ mixed ☐ negative ☐ very negative

Which of the following best describes your attitude toward the idea of meeting your victim?
☐ very positive ☐ positive ☐ mixed ☐ negative ☐ very negative

Do you care about what the victim thinks of you?
☐ yes ☐ no

Of the following items, which is the most important to your thinking about fairness in the justice system?
☐ punishing the offender ☐ having the offender personally make things right
☐ paying back the victim ☐ allowing the offender to apologize to the victim
☐ getting help for the offender ☐ allowing the offender to apologize to his/her family

Given your understanding of fairness, did you experience fairness within the justice system in your case?
☐ yes ☐ no

How was your case eventually disposed of? _____

Is there anything else you would like to say about how your case was handled by the justice system?
_____
_____

THANK YOU VERY MUCH FOR PARTICIPATING IN THIS RESEARCH.

Appendix 125

VICTIM QUESTIONNAIRE

(Please indicate your answer to the following questions and return this form in the enclosed envelope to Cpt. Stahr, Bethlehem Police Department, 10 E. Church Street, Bethlehem, PA 18018. YOUR OPINION MATTERS! Thank you.)

Name of offender: _____

Type of offense: _____ today's date _____

Description of offense: _____

victim's age _____ ☐ male ☐ female ☐ white ☐ black ☐ Hispanic ☐ other (specify)_____

How satisfied were you with the way the justice system handled your case?
☐ very satisfied ☐ satisfied ☐ dissatisfied ☐ very dissatisfied

Do you believe that your opinion regarding the offense and offender was adequately considered in this case?
☐ yes ☐ no

Do you believe the offender was adequately held accountable for his/her behavior?
☐ yes ☐ no

For the following items, please indicate if the item is very important, important, unimportant or very unimportant.

To receive answers to questions you would like to ask the offender.
☐ very important ☐ important ☐ unimportant ☐ very unimportant

To tell the offender how the offense affected you.
☐ very important ☐ important ☐ unimportant ☐ very unimportant

To get paid back for your losses by the offender.
☐ very important ☐ important ☐ unimportant ☐ very unimportant

To see that the offender gets some counseling or other type of help.
☐ very important ☐ important ☐ unimportant ☐ very unimportant

To have the offender punished.
☐ very important ☐ important ☐ unimportant ☐ very unimportant

To have the offender say he/she is sorry.
☐ very important ☐ important ☐ unimportant ☐ very unimportant

To have the opportunity to negotiate a repayment agreement with the offender that is acceptable to you both.
☐ very important ☐ important ☐ unimportant ☐ very unimportant

---

Do you think that a structured meeting with the offender might be helpful?
☐ not at all helpful ☐ somewhat helpful ☐ very helpful

Which of the following best describes your attitude toward the offender at this point in time?
☐ very positive ☐ positive ☐ mixed ☐ negative ☐ very negative

Are you afraid the offender will commit another crime against you?
☐ yes ☐ no

How do you now feel about the offense committed against you?
☐ very upset ☐ somewhat upset ☐ not upset

Of the following items, which is the most important to your thinking about fairness in the justice system?
☐ punishing the offender ☐ having the offender personally make things right
☐ paying back the victim ☐ allowing the offender to apologize to the victim
☐ getting help for the offender ☐ allowing the offender to apologize to his/her family

Given your understanding of fairness, did you experience fairness within the justice system in your case?
☐ yes ☐ no

Is there anything else you would like to say about how your case was handled by the justice system?

_____

_____

THANK YOU VERY MUCH FOR PARTICIPATING IN THIS RESEARCH.

case# _____

PARENT'S QUESTIONNAIRE

Date of court hearing: ___/___/___   Today's date: ___/___/___

Please indicate your answer to the following questions and return this form in the attached envelope to Cpt. Stahr, Bethlehem Police Department, 10 E. Church Street, Bethlehem, PA 18018. YOUR OPINION MATTERS! Thank you.

1. How satisfied were you with the way your child's case was handled?
   ___ very satisfied   ___ satisfied   ___ dissatisfied   ___ very dissatisfied

2. Do you believe your child was adequately held accountable for the offense committed?
   ___ yes ___ no

3. Were you surprised by anything that occurred in the court session?   ___ yes ___ no
   3a. IF YES: By what?
   ___ it went better than I expected   ___ the victim(s) seemed to care about my child
   ___ it was worse than I expected   ___ the victim(s) was so angry
   ___ other: specify _____

4. For the following, please indicate how important each item is to you:
   To be able to tell the victim(s) how you felt.
   ___ very important   ___ important   ___ unimportant   ___ very unimportant
   To be able to tell your child how you felt.
   ___ very important   ___ important   ___ unimportant   ___ very unimportant
   To have the opportunity to work out an agreement with the victim(s) that was acceptable to everyone.
   ___ very important   ___ important   ___ unimportant   ___ very unimportant
   To be able to apologize to the victim(s) for what my child did.
   ___ very important   ___ important   ___ unimportant   ___ very unimportant
   To have my child apologize for what he/she did.
   ___ very important   ___ important   ___ unimportant   ___ very unimportant

5. Was payment or community service ordered during the court session?   ___ yes ___ no
   5a. IF YES: restitution $ _____
                 fine $ _____
   community service (No. Hours) _____

   5b. IF YES: Was this fair to you?   ___ yes ___ no
               Was this fair to your child?   ___ yes ___ no
               Was this fair to the victim(s)? ___ yes ___ no

6. Which of the following best describes your attitude toward your child now?
   ___ very positive   ___ positive   ___ mixed   ___ negative   ___ very negative

7. Do you think the victim(s) has a better opinion of your child after court?   ___ yes ___ no

8. Do you have a better opinion of your child after court?   ___ yes ___ no

9. How likely do you think it is that your child will commit another similar offense?
   - ☐ very likely ☐ likely ☐ unlikely ☐ very unlikely

10. Do you think that a meeting with the victim might be helpful?
    - ☐ not at all helpful ☐ somewhat helpful ☐ very helpful

11. Would you feel nervous about a structured meeting with the victim attended by your child, friends and family?
    - ☐ yes ☐ no

12. Which of the following best describes your attitude toward the victim(s) now?
    - ☐ very positive ☐ positive ☐ mixed ☐ negative ☐ very negative

13. Which of the following best describes your attitude toward meeting the victim?
    - ☐ very positive ☐ positive ☐ mixed ☐ negative ☐ very negative

14. Do you believe that your opinion regarding the offense and circumstances was adequately considered in this case? ☐ yes ☐ no

15. Given your understanding of fairness, did you experience fairness in your case? ☐ yes ☐ no

16. Of the following items, which is the most important to your thinking about fairness in the justice system?
    - ☐ punishing the offender
    - ☐ paying back the victim
    - ☐ getting help for the offender
    - ☐ having the offender personally make things right
    - ☐ allowing the offender to apologize to the victim
    - ☐ allowing the offender to apologize to his/her family

17. How was this case eventually disposed of? _____

18. Is there anything else you would like to say about how your child's case was handled?

_____
_____
_____
_____
_____
_____
_____

THANK YOU VERY MUCH FOR PARTICIPATING IN THIS RESEARCH.

CONFERENCE OBSERVATION SHEET

Observer: Paul Ben Other   case number: _____

Coordinator: _____   Offense: _____

date: _____ time begin: _____ a.m./p.m. time end: _____ a.m./p.m. soc time: _____ a.m./p.m.

- [ ] Introductions
- [ ] Permission for observers
- [ ] Appreciation of effort
- [ ] Set conference focus
- [ ] Offender right to terminate
- [ ] Check for understanding
- [ ] Stay with offender appropriately

avoidance of emotion	
use of silence	
refocus discussion	
failure to refocus	
interrupt participant	
redundant question	

	Offender	Victim	Victim Supporters	Offender Supporters	Coordinator
respect for offender					
respect for victim					
disapproval of act					
disapproval of offender					
offender apologizes					
offender is forgiven					
offender is defiant					
consequences of act					
suggest reparation to victim					
suggest reparation to community					

COORDINATOR

Did the officer maintain the distinction between person and behavior?
not at all |—————|—————|—————|—————|—————| completely

Was any reparation suggested by the officer?
not at all |—————|—————|—————|—————|—————| completely

Was the reparation outcome affected by the officer?
not at all |—————|—————|—————|—————|—————| completely

Did the officer "lecture" the offender?
never |—————|—————|—————|—————|—————| all the time

To what extent did the officer adhere to conference coordination protocol?
not at all |—————|—————|—————|—————|—————| completely

VICTIM

Did the victim seem satisfied with the outcome?
not at all |—————|—————|—————|—————|—————| completely

Did the victim indicate a sense of forgiveness?
not at all |—————|—————|—————|—————|—————| completely

OFFENDER

Did the offender appear to understand the injury caused to the victim?
not at all |—————|—————|—————|—————|—————| completely

Did the offender seem to express sincere remorse?
not at all |—————|—————|—————|—————|—————| completely

Did the offender appear to end with a feeling of pride?
not at all |—————|—————|—————|—————|—————| completely

OTHER PARTICIPANTS

Did the offender's family volunteer future responsibility for the offender?
not at all |—————|—————|—————|—————|—————| completely

Did the offender's other supporters volunteer future responsibility for the offender?
not at all |—————|—————|—————|—————|—————| completely

Was there a strong sense of reconciliation (reintegration)?
not at all |—————|—————|—————|—————|—————| completely

Which participant seemed most punitive? _____

Was restitution from the offender agreed to?

☐ no   ☐ yes   ☐ money   *amount total* $ _____   *amount monthly* $ _____
                 ☐ personal service   *total hours* _____
                 ☐ community service   *total hours* _____
                 ☐ other: specify _____

Was action proposed to prevent future similar injuries?
☐ no   ☐ yes: *describe* _____

Was a follow-up plan agreed to?
☐ no   ☐ yes: *describe* _____

Other deviations from protocol _____

Police Attitudes Scales and Items

Crime Control Orientation
(strongly disagree—disagree—no opinion—agree—strongly agree)
• If police officers in high crime areas had fewer restrictions on their use of force, many of the serious crime problems in those neighborhoods would be greatly reduced.
• Police officers would be more effective if they didn't have to worry about "probable cause" requirements for searching citizens.
• Police officers must sometimes use unethical means to accomplish enforcement of the law.
• Many of the decisions by the Supreme Court interfere with the ability of police to fight crime.
• Sometimes police are justified using "questionable practices" to achieve good ends.

Service Orientation
(strongly disagree—disagree—no opinion—agree—strongly agree)
Police officers should assist citizens who are locked out of their cars.
• Police should assist sick or injured persons.
• Police should handle public nuisance problems.
• If police officers act in a service capacity, this detracts from their ability to fight crime.
• Policing should be seen as service organization.
• Police officers should not have to handle calls that involve social or personal problems where no crime is involved.

Perception of Community Support
(strongly disagree—disagree—no opinion—agree—strongly agree)
• The likelihood of a police officer being physically assaulted in Bethlehem is very high.
• Most of the time the media treat police fairly.
• Most people in Bethlehem lack the appropriate level of respect for police.
• Most young people in Bethlehem respect police officers.

Perception of Community Cooperation
(1-100%)
• Percent of citizens in Bethlehem willing to call the police if they see something suspicious.
• Percent of citizens in Bethlehem willing to press charges in minor crimes.
• Percent of citizens in Bethlehem willing to press charges in serious crimes.
• Percent of citizens in Bethlehem willing to report a crime to police if they are victimized.

Belief in Police Discretion
(strongly disagree—disagree—no opinion—agree—strongly agree)
• Police officers should be able to decide whether or not to enforce laws.
• Patrol officers on the street are more effective if they are able to decide on their own when to enforce particular laws.

Perception of Criminal Justice System Support
(very poor—inadequate—adequate—good—outstanding)
• How would you rate the support of the local courts for your police department?
• How would you rate the cooperation of the Lehigh prosecutor's office with your department?
• How would you rate the cooperation of the Northampton prosecutor's office with your department?

Belief in the Quality of Police Services
(very poor—inadequate—adequate—good—outstanding)
• How would you rate the quality of police services provided by your police department?
• How would the residents rate the quality of police services provided by your police department?

Orientation Toward Force
(strongly disagree—disagree—no opinion—agree—strongly agree)
• Police officers should be allowed to use chokeholds.
• Police officers should only able to use deadly force when someone's life is in danger.
• When a police officer is accused of using too much force, only other police officers are qualified to judge.
• Police officers should be allowed to use stun guns.

Orientation Toward Police Solidarity
(strongly disagree—disagree—no opinion—agree—strongly agree)
• I would report a fellow officer for violating a citizen's civil rights.
• I would report a fellow officer for using unnecessary force (e.g. hitting, kicking, punching) when making an arrest.
• I would arrest a fellow officer for driving while intoxicated.
• I would give a fellow officer a speeding ticket.

Police Hassles and Uplifts Scales and Items

Hassle items: "Please indicate the degree to which each experience below <u>hassled or bothered</u> you during the <u>past month</u> as a result of police work."

Uplift items: "Please indicate the degree to which each experience below made you <u>feel good</u> as a result of police work during the <u>past month</u>."

(5-point scale: definitely does not apply to me <—> strongly applies to me)

Organizational Hassles

Communication
- Lack of honesty about my work by superiors
- Interference in my decisions by others
- Having no say in decisions that affect me
- Not receiving recognition for a job well done
- Responsibility without authority to make decisions
- Not being able to speak my mind

Morale
- Feelings of having to conform to "pressure" from peers
- Station instability
- Low morale
- Personality clashes at work

Coworkers
- Problems with coworkers
- Disagreement about how to do something
- Working with people who are inconsiderate
- Working with people who do not listen
- Working with people who are not suited for police work
- Working with people who lack professionalism
- Other members not pulling their weight

Rating
- Unfair promotional policy
- Unfair rating system

Supervision
- Too much supervision
- Being told what to do by others

Administration
- Poor administration
- Inconsistent application of rules and policy
- Inability to change the system
- Lack of clarity in operational guidelines
- Unnecessary forms
- Excessive paperwork
- Lack of forward planning
- Too much red tape to get something done
- Inappropriate rules and regulations

Individual
- Concerns about the status of police
- Feelings of not being able to do anything
- Feeling generally inadequate
- Feelings of just being a number
- Difficulty staying objective (not expressing my emotions)
- "Bottling up" my feelings

Amenities
- Dirty mess rooms
- Poor facilities
- Untidy work areas

Equipment
- Lack of equipment
- Equipment failure

Promotions
- Exams (for work purposes)
- Studying (for work purposes)

<u>Operational Hassles</u>

Danger
- Going to dangerous calls
- Having to make a forcible arrest
- Going on a raid

Victims
- Dealing with abused children
- Taking a road accident report
- Dealing with assault victims
- Giving bad news
- Delivering a death message
- Seeing other people in misery
- Dealing with domestics
- Dealing with road victims

Frustration
- Dealing with people who abuse the police
- Not being able to get an admission from someone who is guilty
- Not being able to charge someone who is guilty
- Doing things I don't agree with
- Doing work I don't like
- Hoax calls

External
- Courts setting inconvenient dates
- Unreasonable expectations from others outside the department
- Outside interference with police work
- Court decisions being too lenient
- Poor media coverage
- Lack of police powers
- Wasting time at court

Activity
- Quick change overs
- Rushed eating
- Irregular meal times
- Missing meals
- Shift work interfering with other activities
- Sitting around then suddenly active

Complaints
- Departmental handling of complaints
- Complaints by the public

People
- Trying to show interest in people
- Dealing with other people's problems
- Being responsible for others

Workload
- Meeting deadlines
- Too much expected of me
- Insufficient time to complete a job
- Too much work to do

Driving
- Poor drivers on road
- Heavy traffic

Organizational Uplifts

Amenities
- Good facilities
- Tidy mess room
- Tidy work area

Coworkers
- Working with people who are considerate
- Working with people who know what they are doing
- Working with people who listen
- Getting along with peers
- Working with people I like
- Working with good performers
- Personal reaction from other officers
- Other officers doing the right thing

Administration
- Clarity of operational guidelines
- Results of my plans taking effect
- Application of rules and policy

Decision-making
- Having a say in decisions
- Making popular decisions
- Accepting responsibility
- Solving a problem
- Making tough decisions

Supervision
- Having someone to turn to for help or advice
- Honesty about my work by superiors
- Helpful supervision

Workload
- Meeting deadlines
- Getting things done
- Working hard
- Achieving a heavy workload

Equipment
- Equipment being available
- Equipment working

Family
- Support for my work from my partner
- Sufficient time with family

Promotions
- Getting a good job
- Receiving a good performance rating
- Opportunity for promotion
- Receiving a good promotions rating

Operational Uplifts

Offenders
- Obtaining an admission from a crook
- Charging someone
- Getting a good result at court
- Going to good calls
- Getting a good "pinch"
- Going on a raid

Victims
- Helping children
- Helping complainants
- Delivering good news
- Public showing interest in my work
- Helping motorists
- Helping the public
- Receiving thanks from the public

Rosters
- Days off
- Good roster
- Shift work fitting in with other activities

Endnotes

Bayley, D.H. (1994) International difference in community policing. In D.P. Rosenbaum (ed.). *The Challenge of Community Policing: Testing the Promises* (pp.278-81). Thousand Oaks, CA: Sage Publications.

Braithwaite, J. (1989) *Crime, Shame and Reintegration.* New York: Cambridge University Press.

Braithwaite, J. (1997) Restorative justice: Assessing an immodest theory and a pessimistic theory. Draft to be submitted to *Crime and Justice: A Review of Research.*

Braithwaite, J. (1994) Thinking harder about democratising social control. In C. Alder & J. Wundersitz (eds.). *Family Conferencing and Juvenile Justice: The Way Forward or Misplaced Optimism?* (pp.199-216). Canberra, Australia: Australian Institute of Criminology.

Brooks, L.W. Piquero, A. & Cronin, J. (1993) Police officer attitudes concerning their communities and their roles: A comparison of two suburban police departments. *American Journal of Police.* 12(3): 115-39.

Bull, D. and Stratta, E. (1994) Police community consultation: An examination of its practice in selected constabularies in England and New South Wales, Australia. *Australian and New Zealand Journal of Criminology.* 27(3): 237-49.

Coates, R. (1985) *Victim Meets Offender: An Evaluation of Victim-offender Reconciliation Programs.* Valparaiso, IN: PACT Institute of Justice.

Coates, R.B. & Gehm, J. (1989) An empirical assessment. In M. Wright & B. Galaway (eds.). *Mediation and Criminal Justice* (pp.251-63). London, UK: Sage.

Couper, D.C. & Lobitz, S.H. (1991) *Quality Policing: The Madison Experience.* Washington, DC: Police Executive Research Forum.

Dignan, J. (1992) Repairing the damage: Can reparation work in the service of diversion? *British Journal of Criminology.* 32:453-72.

Gaines, L. (1994) Community-oriented policing: management issues, concerns, and problems. *Journal of Contemporary Criminal Justice.* 10(1):17-35.

Galaway, B. (1992) The New Zealand experience implementing the reparation sentence. In H. Messmer and H.U. Otto (eds.). *Restorative Justice on Trial: Pitfalls and Potentials of Victim-Offender Mediation* (pp.55-80). Boston: Kluwer Academic Publishers.

Goldstein, H. (1997) Interview in *Law Enforcement News.* 23(461): 8-11.

Goldstein, H. (1990) *Problem-Oriented Policing.* Philadelphia: Temple University Press.

Goldstein, H. (1987) Toward community-oriented policing: potential, basic requirements, and threshold questions. *Crime and Delinquency.* 33(1): 6-30.

Graham, I. (1993) Juvenile justice in New South Wales: New directions. In L. Atkinson & S-A. Gerull (eds.). *National Conference on Juvenile Justice* (pp.149-66). Conference proceedings, no.22. Canberra, Australia: Australian Institute of Criminology.

Haley, J. & Neugebauer, A.M. (1992) Victim-offender mediations: Japanese and American comparisons. In H. Messmer and H.U. Otto (eds.). *Restorative Justice on Trial: Pitfalls and Potentials of Victim-Offender Mediation* (pp.105-30). Boston: Kluwer Academic Publishers.

Hart, P.M., Wearing, A.J. & Headey, B. (1993) Assessing police work experiences: Development of the police daily hassles and uplifts scales. *Journal of Criminal Justice.* 21(6): 553-72.

Hart, P.M., Wearing, A.J. & Headey, B. (1994) Perceived quality of life, personality, and work experiences: Construct validation of the police daily hassles and uplifts scales. *Criminal Justice and Behavior.* 21(3): 283-311.

Hunter, R.D. and Barker, T. (1993) BS and buzzwords: The new police operational style. *American Journal of Police.* 12(3): 157-8.

Iivari, J. (1992) The process of mediation in Finland: A special reference to the question 'How to get cases for mediation'. In H. Messmer and H.U. Otto (eds.). *Restorative Justice on Trial: Pitfalls and Potentials of Victim-Offender Mediation* (pp.137-48). Boston: Kluwer Academic Publishers.

Jones, T., Newburn, T. and Smith, D.J. (1994) *Democracy and Policing.* London, UK: Policy Studies Institute.

Karmen, A. (1990) *Crime Victims: An Introduction to Victimology*, 2nd edition. Belmont, CA: Wadsworth Publishing.

Klockars, C.B. (1988) The rhetoric of community policing. In J.R. Greene and S.D. Mastrofski (eds.). *Community Policing: Rhetoric or Reality* (pp.239-58). New York: Praeger.

Koch, J.R. & Bennett, T. (1993) Community policing in Canada and Britain. Home Office Research and Statistics Department. *Research Bulletin.* 34: 36-42.

Lurigio, A.J. & Skogan, W.G. (1994) Winning the hearts and minds of police officers: An assessment of perceptions of community policing in Chicago. *Crime and Delinquency.* 40(3): 315-30.

Marshall, T.F. (1994) Grassroots initiatives towards restorative justice: The new paradigm? In A. Duff, S. Marshall, R.E. Dobash, et al. (eds.). *Penal Theory and Practice: Tradition and Innovation in Criminal Justice* (pp.245-62). Fulbright papers, volume 15. Manchester, UK: Manchester University Press.

Marshall, T.F. (1992) Restorative justice on trial in Britain. In H. Messmer and H.U. Otto (eds.). *Restorative Justice on Trial: Pitfalls and Potentials of Victim-Offender Mediation* (pp.15-28). Boston: Kluwer Academic Publishers.

Mastrofski, S.D. (1988) Community policing as reform: A cautionary tale. In J.R. Greene and S.D. Mastrofski (eds.). *Community Policing: Rhetoric or Reality* (pp.47-68). New York: Praeger.

McCold, P. (1997a) *Restorative Justice: An Annotated Bibliography.* Monsey, NY: Criminal Justice Press.

McCold, P. (1997b, May) Restorative justice: variations on a theme. Paper presented at the Restorative Justice for Juveniles: Potentialities, Risks and Problems for Research, International Conference, Leuven, Belgium.

McCold, P. (1996) The role of community in restorative justice. In B. Galaway and J. Hudson (eds.) *Restorative Justice: International Perspectives* (pp.85-102). Monsey, NY: Criminal Justice Press.

McCold, P. & Wachtel, B. (1998) Community is not a place: A new look at community justice initiatives. Forthcoming in *Contemporary Justice Review.* 1(1).

McDonald, J., Moore, D., O'Connell, T. & Thorsborne, M. (1995) <u>REAL JUSTICE</u> *Training Manual: Coordinating Family Group Conferences*. Pipersville, PA: The Piper's Press.

Moore, D.B. (1995) *A New Approach to Juvenile Justice: An Evaluation of Family Conferencing in Wagga Wagga*. A report to the Criminology Research Council. Wagga Wagga, Australia: Centre for Rural Social Research, Charles Sturt University-Riverina.

Moore, D.B. (1993) Shame, forgiveness, and juvenile justice. *Criminal Justice Ethics*. 12(1): 3-25.

Moore, D.B. & McDonald, J.M. (1995) Achieving the 'Good Community': A local police initiative and its wider ramifications. In K.M. Hazlehurst (ed.). *Perceptions of Justice: Issues in Indigenous and Community Empowerment* (pp.143-73). Brookfield, VT: Ashgate Publishing.

Moore, D.B. & O'Connell, T. (1994) Family conferencing in Wagga Wagga: A communitarian model of justice. In C. Alder & J. Wundersitz (eds.). *Family Conferencing and Juvenile Justice: The Way Forward or Misplaced Optimism?* (pp.45-86). Canberra, Australia: Australian Institute of Criminology.

Nelligan, P.J. & Taylor, R.W. (1994) Ethical issues in community policing. *Journal of Contemporary Criminal Justice*. 10(1): 59-66.

Normandeau, A. (1993) Community policing in Canada: A review of some recent studies. *American Journal of Police*. 12(1): 57-73.

Overman, R., Carey, L.R. & Dolan, H.P. (1994) The case for community policing. *Police Chief*. 61(3): 20-32.

Pate, K. (1990) Victim-offender restitution programs in Canada. In B. Galaway and J. Hudson (eds.). *Criminal Justice, Restitution and Reconciliation* (pp.135-44). Monsey, NY: Willow Tree Press.

Redlinger, L.J. (1994) Community policing and changes in the organizational structure. *Journal of Contemporary Criminal Justice*. 10(1): 36-57.

Riechers, L.M. & Roberg, R.R. (1990) Community policing: A critical review of underlying assumptions. *Journal of Police Science and Administration*. 17(2): 105-14.

Rosenbaum, D.P. & Lurigio, A. (1994) Community policing. *Crime and Delinquency*. 40(3): 299-468.

Sherman, L. (1996, November) Randomizing shame to criminal events: issues in experimental criminology. Paper presented at the American Society of Criminology Conference, annual meeting, Chicago.

Sherman, L. & Barnes, G.C. (1997, April) Restorative justice and offenders' respect for the law. RISE working paper #2. Australia National University.

Sherman, L. & Strang, H. (1997a, April) The right kind of shame from crime prevention. RISE working paper #1. Australia National University.

Sherman, L. & Strang, H. (1997b, April) Restorative justice and deterring crime. RISE working paper #4. Australia National University.

Skolnick, J.H. & Bayley, D.H. (1988) Theme and variation in community policing. In M. Tonry & N. Morris (eds.). *Crime and Justice: A Review of Research*. 10: 1-38.

Stenson, K. (1993) Community policing as a governmental technology. *Economy and Society*. 22(3): 373-89.

Strang, H. (1997, November) Restorative justice for victims of juvenile offenders. Paper presented at the American Society of Criminology, annual meeting, San Diego.

Strang, H. & Sherman, L. (1997, April).The victim's perspective. RISE working paper #3. Australia National University.

Trenczek, T. (1990) A review and assessment of victim-offender reconciliation programming in West Germany. In B. Galaway and J. Hudson (eds.). *Criminal Justice, Restitution and Reconciliation* (pp.109-24). Monsey, NY: Willow Tree Press.

Umbreit, M.S. (1994) *Victim Meets Offender: The Impact of Restorative Justice and Mediation.* Monsey, NY: Willow Tree Press.

Umbreit, M.S. (1996) Mediation of criminal conflict: An assessment of programs in four Canadian provinces. In B. Galaway & J. Hudson (eds.). *Restorative Justice: International Perspectives* (pp.373-86). Monsey, NY: Criminal Justice Press.

Umbreit, M.S. & Roberts, A.W. (1996) *Mediation of Criminal Conflict in England: An Assessment of Services in Coventry and Leeds.* Center for Restorative Justice & Mediation. St. Paul, MN: University of Minnesota.

Umbreit, M. & Zehr, H. (1996) Family group conferences: A challenge to victim-offender mediation? *VOMA Quarterly.* 7(1): 4-8.

Van Ness, D. & Strong, K. (1997) *Restoring Justice.* Cincinnati: Anderson Publishing Company.

Wachtel, T. (1995) Family group conferencing: restorative justice in practice. *Juvenile Justice Update.* 1(4):1-2, 13-14.

Walker, S. (1993) Does anyone remember team policing? Lessons of team policing experience for community policing. *American Journal of Police.* 12(4): 33-55.

Weisburd, D. & Green, L. (1995) Measuring immediate spatial displacement: methodological issues and problems. In J. Eck & D. Weisburd (eds.). *Crime and Place* (pp.349-63). Monsey, NY: Criminal Justice Press.

Wright, M. (1996). *Justice for Victims and Offenders: A Restorative Response to Crime,* 2nd edition. Winchester, UK: Waterside Press.

Wundersitz, J. & Hetzel, S. (1996) Family conferencing for young offenders: The South Australian experience. In J. Hudson, A. Morris, G. Maxwell & B. Galaway (eds.). *Family Group Conferences: Perspectives on Policy and Practice* (pp.111-39). Monsey, NY: Willow Tree Press.

Zehr, H. (1990) *Changing Lenses: A New Focus for Crime and Justice.* Scottsdale, PA: Herald Press.

Zhao, J., Thurman, J.C. & Lovrich, N.P. (1995) Community-oriented policing across the U.S.: Facilitators and impediment to implementation. *American Journal of Police.* 14(1): 11-28.